Praise for Becoming a Succe

"The authors make an anatomical evaluation of the practical dos and don'ts to becoming an outstanding manager. They create a powerful, easy-to-read text that will benefit managers at all levels. For organizations seeking to create competitive advantage through people development, the tenets and practical suggestions put forward become a living process and mandatory reading."

Dorset Sutton
Vice President/Managing Director
South East Asia Region
Colgate-Palmolive

"This is a great book for new managers! It provides effective tips, especially in delivering constructive criticism, conducting interviews, and running meetings. I recommend it as mandatory reading."

Joan Gundlach
Vice President, Affiliate Sales
Central Region
A&E Television Networks

"Invaluable help for every new manager and a practical step-by-step guide to achieving managerial success. A perfect refresher for any seasoned manager and a must for every corporate training department. A remarkable book."

Arthur Coren
Former Chairman and CEO
Zenith Controls, Inc.

"This book identifies and deals with key issues of transitioning to a business leadership role. Readers will recognize that the authors have been where they are going and will want to learn from their experience. . . . brings essential advice to the next generation of leaders."

Rodger De Rose
Former Partner
Arthur Andersen

"This is the best book I've ever read on how to be a great manager. It should be required reading for all new managers and would make an outstanding refresher course for seasoned professionals. It's full of practical insights, helpful examples, and all the right values. I plan on recommending it widely."

Tom Morris
Morris Institute for Human Values
Author of *True Success* and
If Aristotle Ran General Motors

"This practical and useful guide for new managers will transform mediocre managers into outstanding ones. All managers should have a copy to help launch their careers and to refer back to once they've learned the ropes."

Stephen J. Kinner
Senior Vice President
Director Sales and Marketing
Federal Home Loan Bank
of Des Moines

"Straightforward advice that encourages development of the fundamental people skills that earned the manager his or her promotion in the first place. Provides the new manager with the tools needed to handle all work experiences from harassment issues to conducting efficient and motivational meetings. A great book for all levels of management!"

James P. Grusecki
Chairman and
Chief Executive Officer
Northern Builders, Inc.

Becoming
a *Successful*
Manager

How to Make
a Smooth Transition
from Managing Yourself
to Managing Others

Jack H. Grossman, Ph.D., and J. Robert Parkinson, Ph.D.

Contemporary Books

Chicago   New York   San Francisco   Lisbon   London   Madrid   Mexico City
Milan   New Delhi   San Juan   Seoul   Singapore   Sydney   Toronto

Library of Congress Cataloging-in-Publication Data

Grossman, Jack H.
    Becoming a successful manager : how to make a smooth transition from
managing yourself to managing others / Jack H. Grossman and J. Robert
Parkinson.
        p.   cm.
    ISBN 0-658-01489-7
    1. Executive ability.   2. Self-management (Psychology)   3. Interpersonal
relations.   4. Employee motivation.   5. Management.   I. Parkinson, J.
Robert (John Robert)   II. Title.

HD38.2 .G76   2001
658.4'09—dc21   2001037284

Contemporary Books

A Division of The **McGraw·Hill** Companies

    5 6 7 8 9 0   VBA/VBA   0 9 8 7 6

ISBN 0-658-01489-7

This book was set in Plantin
Printed and bound by Maple-Vail Book Manufacturing Group

Cover design by Monica Baziuk
Interior design by Amy Yu Ng

McGraw-Hill books are available at special quantity discounts to use as premiums and
sales promotions, or for use in corporate training programs. For more information, please
write to the Director of Special Sales, Professional Publishing, McGraw-Hill, Two Penn
Plaza, New York, NY 10121-2298. Or contact your local bookstore.

This book is printed on acid-free paper.

To Joan, of course, my wife and friend for forty-five years, and to my loving family.

—J.H.G.

To Eileen, wife and partner for four decades. It just doesn't seem possible that so much time has passed.

—J.R.P.

Contents

   - *What I Get Paid to Do*
   - *Essentials for Managerial Excellence*
   - *The Three Elements of Attitudes*
   - *Encourage Positive Attitudes*
   - *Being an Excellent Manager Begins with
     Being a Good Person—a Mensch*
   - *How Do You Make Your Employees Feel?*
   - *The Problem-Solving Process*
   - *Characteristics of a Departmental Weed*

Acknowledgments

THERE ARE SO MANY PEOPLE TO thank for contributing to the production of this text that it is difficult to know where to start. First, we must thank all of the managers with whom we have been associated throughout our professional careers. They provided much of the research material that made this endeavor possible. Next, we owe a great deal to our literary agent, Joelle Delbourgo, who led us through the rigors of finding the right publisher. And finally, a heartfelt thanks to our editor, Denise Betts, for her guidance in directing us from having a good idea to producing a good book.

A Note from
the Authors

THE PURPOSE OF THIS BOOK IS to help you, as a new manager, quickly assimilate some of the basic knowledge you must have and actions you must put into practice in order to succeed. For you to gain maximum benefit from the material, we recommend that you keep a manager's journal. In it, note the thoughts, ideas, and insights you generate while reading. A manager's journal is also an excellent place to record your completed exercises, which are presented throughout these chapters, as well as other useful reminders and information that will help you become the outstanding manager you have the potential to be.

Introduction
How You Can Benefit
from This Book

CONGRATULATIONS ON BEING PROMOTED TO MANAGER! By accepting this promotion, you assumed three essential and overlapping responsibilities: to become a professional manager, to get people of diverse backgrounds and skills to fulfill their individual and departmental objectives, and to create a spirit of professionalism and teamwork within your department.

As you probably realize, achieving these objectives is an arduous job. Managing a department effectively is an ongoing process that consists of developing mutually rewarding relationships with your employees. You will be required to create healthy partnerships with each of the people under your influence. The basic ingredients of all such committed relationships are the same: mutual respect and trust spiced with genuine caring attitudes and feelings.

You know you've successfully created healthy manager-employee relationships when your employees feel that the department belongs to them as well as to you. That feeling, in all likelihood, will motivate them to be vital contributors to the department and will discourage them from the subtle ways in which disgruntled or dissatisfied employees can hinder departmental development. Once a genuine team spirit evolves and bonding occurs, you, your employees, and the organization for which you work will profit in every way—emotionally, intellectually, and ultimately financially.

Since you are your department's manager, you must spearhead the formation of such partnerships. You must also do everything in your power to preserve the integrity of each of your manager-employee relationships, and protect that integrity from being threatened or invaded by negative staff members or negative workplace situations. Difficult as it may be to create and uphold the partnerships between you and your employees, that's what you must do to succeed as a professional manager.

In order to achieve the status of professional manager, you must take the following actions: You must assume responsibility for creating a fertile workplace culture—an atmosphere that stimulates people of diverse abilities, personalities, and backgrounds to be productive and to work harmoniously with one another. (You know your departmental culture is fertile when its members contribute willingly, enthusiastically, and fully toward your—and their—department's common causes.) You must make it safe for people in your department to communicate openly and nondefensively with you and each other, and to take intellectual risks without fear of repercussions. You must create a structure that allows people to develop and grow into their fullest potential. Finally, you must be the inspiration and guiding force that leads your department forward.

These are tall orders, but they are, in part, the responsibilities you assumed when you donned the mantle of manager. When you accepted this position, your implied promise, assuming you want to be the best leader you can be, was to be an effective teacher, a sensitive counselor, and a master gardener. A professional and successful manager assumes all three roles.

Before we examine the nature of these roles, we will discuss what it means to be a professional manager—or, for that matter, a professional in any occupation—and what distinguishes professionals from nonprofessionals. The distinction between professionals and nonprofessionals is based on more than results achieved or whether or not they get paid for their work. Rather, the basic differences between the two concern how they approach their work, how they interact with their clients or customers, and how they present themselves to the world.

Professionals Versus Nonprofessionals

Professionals know what they're doing and are in full control of their domain. This control, which stems in part from professionals' thorough knowledge of their areas of expertise, enables them to execute responsibilities with utmost confidence. Conveying a true image of quiet strength, they engender trust from the people under their influence. Conversely, nonprofessionals are unsure of themselves, in part because they lack the knowledge and experience to be surefooted. This lack of confidence in what they're doing causes them to be defensive when their decisions are questioned. Ultimately, the nonprofessionals' lack of confidence, defensive nature, and apparent lack of complete control over their domain cause others to distrust them and their judgments. Such conditions inevitably create chaos and a negative work environment.

Professionals focus their energies on fulfilling their responsibilities and achieving results, not on portraying a particular image. Because professionals believe that their actions, performance, and accomplishments speak for themselves, the positive image others have of them is based on tangible results, not on what they say about themselves. Nonprofessionals talk about what they plan to do, but their talk is generally not followed by actions. This is a symptom of their desire to create a favorable image. For nonprofessionals, looking good seems to be of greater concern than actually being good. However, in reality, they don't look good, because they don't follow through on their promises, and as a result, they are frequently criticized for "talking a better game than they play."

Professionals make what they do look easy. This is a result of their awareness of what's required to excel and their dedication to perfecting their skills. Nonprofessionals often struggle to accomplish what is required of them. It's as if they're not sure of themselves and what constitutes appropriate actions, so they muddle along in pursuit of undefined and underdeveloped objectives.

Professionals are subtle when performing their jobs. They fulfill objectives without calling attention to themselves and their activities and without flaunting their position. Recipients of their services know they're benefiting, but they don't know the minutia of what the professional is doing to effect this result. Of professional managers we have known, people in their departments say things like, "I don't know what he does to gain cooperation, but we want to cooperate." Or, "I learn from my manager, but it doesn't seem that she actually teaches."

Professionals in a management position *gain cooperation without domination.* Not only are nonprofessionals obvious about what they do, but also their intentions are transparent and suspect. Because nonprofessionals are motivated mainly by ego rather than the desire to be of service to others, they tend to misuse their authority and power. It's as if they're wearing a shirt emblazoned "I am boss." Of course, people who work for such managers see right through them and either learn to play the manager's childish games or leave the department in disgust.

Professionals walk their talk. Their actions consistently reflect their beliefs and the principles they advocate. While some nonprofessionals may be knowledgeable and may voice sound and lofty beliefs, for the most part, their actions are inconsistent with their stated beliefs. It's as if they are two different people.

Professionals are highly disciplined and, therefore, consistently do what is required in order to move forward. They are motivated by the desire to honor their profession and to excel, and their actions are committed to these objectives. Nonprofessionals are undisciplined and tend to work only when they feel like it. In general, this is because they're not fully committed to fulfilling their stated objectives.

Professionals tend to be task and goal oriented; therefore, their efforts are appropriate and lead to meaningful results. Although they know how to have fun, and they often do, for them frivolity has its time and place. Oftentimes, nonprofessionals allow themselves to get caught up with issues tangential to main objectives. They are frequently accused of not taking seriously the jobs or projects they undertake. They are also inappropriately frivolous and allow themselves to become mired in matters that have nothing to do with attaining meaningful results.

As you can see, professionalism and success as a manager are more than merely titles, credentials, and getting paid well for what one does. They are about a person's demeanor and attitude when dealing with a disparate group of people and properly handling a variety of work-related issues or problems. That being the case, let's talk about the three major roles of a professional manager.

A Professional Manager's Primary Role: Be an Effective Teacher

To be an effective teacher, you must dedicate yourself to expanding your "students'" knowledge, skills, vistas, and problem-solving abilities. Your challenge is to provide them with all the tools and encouragement they need to become independent thinkers and productive contributors to your department. To illustrate how you might go about achieving these results, let's go back in time and identify possible role models. You may want to note your observations in your manager's journal.

First, recall one or two of the best teachers you ever had. Envision them in the classroom, interacting with you and other students. What made these interactions special? Did you look forward to coming to class, and if so, why? What specifically did they consistently do that made such a lasting impression on you?

In all likelihood, whatever impressed you about these teachers stemmed from their eagerness to transmit their knowledge, their desire to help you understand the material they were teaching, and their commitment to stimulating you to think clearly and independently. Chances are that their genuine caring made you feel special and encouraged you to develop a strong interest in what you were learning. Finally, they probably never said or did anything to embarrass you, even when you asked a question that you, and perhaps your classmates, thought was dumb.

In order to be a professional manager, you must exhibit qualities similar to those exemplified by outstanding teachers, but remember: *your success as a manager depends, to a significant degree, on the effectiveness of the collective nonmanagers in your department.* That is why you should do everything within your power to help your employees make the most of their potential. You do that by exercising your power responsibly, just as your great teachers did. Always respond appropriately to questions without making the questioner feel stupid or guilty. And, when it has become clear, through tangible results, that your employees learned what you taught them, reinforce their learning with sincere praise and acknowledgment.

What else can you do to stimulate your "students'" desire and ability to learn and develop? Keep this question in mind while reading the rest of this Introduction. At the end, write down your thoughts, ideas, and insights in your manager's journal. When it's appropriate, put these thoughts into practice, and monitor the results of your actions.

A Professional Manager's Secondary Role: Be a Sensitive Counselor

Companies often get more than they bargain for when they hire someone. While companies hire people for their abilities, intellect, skills, and potential to contribute to the organization, they will also receive each employee's unique attitudes, emotions, and interests. Because employees are people first and producers second, their productivity is affected emotionally by experiences and events both at home and at work. As a professional manager, you have to deal with a range of emotionally charged issues and distorted perceptions that evince anger, sadness, jealousies, upsets, and more. These situations will require you to be a sensitive counselor, which is an integral part of being a professional manager.

In the role of counselor, you are an authority figure whose objective is to listen attentively and sensitively to employees who trust you with their feelings. You then provide alternative courses of action available. By listening nonjudgmentally, you convey the impression that you genuinely care, and your suggested options will be taken seriously. Realize that neither you nor anyone else can solve another person's problems; each of us must assume that responsibility ourselves. However, in acting as a concerned and sensitive counselor, you must invite troubled employees to talk about what is interfering with their effectiveness and then offer options for resolving the difficulty. The goal is not to develop a therapeutic relationship with an employee, as would a psychologist, psychiatrist, or social worker. Rather, you should be able to conduct one or two productive meetings with a troubled employee that address specific behavioral symptoms that have job-related negative consequences.

A Professional Manager's Third Role: Be a Master Gardener

If you ask serious gardeners what the secret to their success is, they'll tell you something along the lines of: "First, I have to create a fertile culture that stimulates healthy plant growth. Next, I must ensure that the different species of plants in the garden are compatible. And finally, I have to maintain the garden by watering, cultivating, weeding, and fertilizing it, and by providing special attention to plants that require it." Master gardeners will also tell you that this is a full-time job yielding great joy when they see the positive results of their efforts.

It doesn't require much of a stretch to apply the rules and principles of successful gardening to being a successful professional manager. The "human plants" you choose to be part of your departmental garden have to reflect your values and be willing to contribute to your vision of what you want your "garden" to produce. Assuming you hire capable, high-potential, and conscientious people, your abilities and skills as a manager will determine how productive and responsive they will be to you. The chance of managing a cooperative team that's full of potential is great if you do your job well.

A significant part of your job is to see to it that "weeds" and other threats to the health of your departmental garden don't drain it of its nutrients or adversely affect employees' morale and productivity. The single most treacherous weed with which you will need to contend is defensiveness.

Helping you fulfill each of these three roles so you can become an excellent professional manager is our aim. Make this book your personal guide for building a solid, long-lasting departmental foundation and healthy structure. By approaching this material as you would an ongoing one-on-one seminar designed just for you, you can realize the implied promise of the book's title. We wish you success in making a graceful transition from managing yourself to managing others!

Questions to Consider

- *Regarding the best teachers you ever had, did you look forward to their classes, and if so, why?*

- *What specifically did they consistently do to make a lasting impression on you?*

- *What specifically can you do to stimulate your employees' abilities to learn and develop?*

- *What specifically can you do that would make your employees look forward to coming to work every day and approach their jobs with enthusiasm?*

PART I

Establishing a Solid Departmental Foundation

If someone were to ask you, "As manager of your department, what is your main overall objective?" you might say something like, "I want to build a strong and productive departmental structure." Few people would argue with that response. It's a goal that is not only reasonable but also achievable. The first step toward achieving your goal is to build a solid foundation, one that can support the departmental structure you want to create.

The cornerstone of such a foundation consists of four essential elements:

- Actions, based on your genuine caring attitudes, that consistently demonstrate respect for your fellow human beings
- Practices, also stemming from genuine caring attitudes, that reflect your trustworthiness, as well as your trust and respect toward your employees
- Values and principles that reflect genuine caring attitudes toward all people whose cooperation you need to succeed
- Sound business principles that reflect concerns for both the financial bottom line and the processes leading to it

How you can build a foundation of which you will be proud is the subject of Chapters 1 through 7. Each chapter either helps you understand the nature of your job as a manager or demonstrates how you can incorporate one or more of the four elements in your foundation. We'll begin by taking a bird's-eye view of what your job actually is—that is, your implied promises and obligations to your employees. In subsequent chapters, you will learn the basics of how to fulfill your obligations.

As you study these seven chapters, keep in mind two key principles you need to follow to be a successful professional manager:

- Strive to create a departmental culture that enables people under your influence to be productive and to grow.
- Surround yourself with people who are trustworthy and whom you respect, both personally and professionally.

Sensitivity is as important to managing people as music is to dancing.

A professional manager is an effective teacher, a sensitive counselor, and a master gardener.

1

Define Your Role

BEFORE YOUR PROMOTION, YOU MANAGED only one person: yourself. In this limited managerial function, your efforts and effectiveness alone determined your success. You must have been good at what you were doing or you wouldn't be in your current position of departmental manager. But your "doing" skills that were once admired and rewarded are not what you get paid for now. Now the rules for succeeding are substantially different.

In your role as departmental manager, your two main responsibilities are to stimulate the members of your staff to be the best they can be and to meld a diverse group of skilled individuals into a cohesive team of people who work well together to accomplish the goals you've been charged to achieve. Your likelihood of fulfilling those two responsibilities will increase if you embody this precept: As a manager, I am only as good as the people under my influence; therefore, helping them become as effective as they can be is my number one priority.

In your managerial position, you are like a master gardener of an estate. Of course, the garden of which you're in charge consists of people, who are considerably more complex than varied flowers and vegetation, but they both require fertile soil as well as proper care and feeding for them to fulfill their potential. Some people, just like exotic flowers, may even require special treatment. Regardless of their differences, what's obvious about both gardens is that neither can ever be taken for granted if it is to flourish.

How to Make Sure Your Garden Flourishes

Because you head the department, all actions and standards of performance must reflect your mission, your values, and your philosophies concerning the way people treat others both within and outside the group. Being your garden's chief architect, you must establish its culture and make sure the people under your influence perpetuate the principles that govern it.

As you embark on your first important project, which is to mold your department's culture, keep in mind a quality common to excellent managers we have known. We call that quality quiet strength.

Managers who possess quiet strength have a positive influence on others without being obvious in their methods. They are clear about what they expect and desire from the people with whom they interact. After making sure their expectations and desires are reasonable, they unobtrusively do what's necessary to achieve both their expectations and their desires.

Their subtle actions, which prompt others to respond favorably to them, reflect genuine caring attitudes that say, in effect, "You are important to me," "I value your contributions," "I respect you and your abilities," and "I trust your judgment."

If in your dealings with your staff you were to adopt such attitudes, you would stimulate your employees to produce results of which you and everyone else in your department would be proud.

In contrast to quiet-strength managers are those who manage by intimidation. Typically, these managers overpower people with their authority. They yell, threaten, pout, talk mean, or do whatever else they can to instill fear in people under their influence. Although they may get short-term results, more often than not, such bullying actions and misuse of authority result in defensive behaviors, which prevent employees from consistently doing their best.

Assuming you want to establish quiet strength as a philosophical foundation for effectively managing your department, ensure all of your employees are aware that you plan to abide by the following three-part code of conduct.

What I Get Paid to Do

- I get paid to create a department in which we all feel motivated to be the best we can be.
- I get paid to encourage everyone to cooperate with one another so we can achieve our department's objectives.
- I get paid to ensure that we all abide by the ideals and standards that define our department.

Frame this reminder, and either hang it in your office for all to see or place it on your desk. (See the Appendix for reproducible text.)

Just as fertile soil is essential for beautiful flowers to grow, a fertile departmental culture is a basic requirement for people to be productive and cooperative. This plaque serves as a reminder of what it takes to create and sustain that culture. At the end of this chapter, under "Questions to Consider," compare what you think you get paid to do with your three-part code.

Create a Departmental Mission Statement

Your company probably has a mission statement that conveys to all of its employees and to the world outside what the purpose of its business is and how it intends to accomplish its objectives. Essentially, this statement is the company's constitution.

Although this document is useful, it is also beneficial to create a departmental mission statement that embodies your ideals—those you would like your employees to embrace. Whether you've inherited the department that you are managing or are responsible for forming a new department, you might want to enlist the help of your staff to develop a mission statement that reflects both your and their ideals.

To be meaningful, the department's mission statement should answer the following questions:

1. What's the ultimate purpose of our department?
2. How will our department accomplish its objectives?
3. How can our department make a difference to the people we serve?
4. What kind of product and/or service would we be pleased to receive if we were the department's customers?
5. What does our department stand for philosophically?

6. What are the standards that our department intends to live by?

7. What makes our department important?

After you and your employees answer these questions, use your responses to arrive at a statement that summarizes your department's reason for being and how you intend to achieve your objectives.

There is no one right way of creating a departmental mission statement, since it's a personal reflection of your values, your ideals, your vision of the department's character, and how you want the department to function.

Once you have arrived at a mission statement that is viable for you and your staff, distribute a copy to each of your employees and request that they review it often.

Consistently Lead by Example

Your staff can view your departmental mission statement as mere words, or it can be taken seriously. Since you want it to be taken seriously, your actions must conform to its dictates. It is demoralizing to people to be managed by someone who is seen as a hypocrite—a person who talks a better game than he or she plays. How can such a person be trusted? How can such a person be respected? To be trusted and respected, you must live your mission statement and strongly encourage your staff to do the same.

The following creed, which you might also want to frame and put on your wall, can guide you in backing up your words with actions. (See the Appendix for reproducible text.) Throughout this book, we elaborate on the eleven essentials it contains.

Essentials for Managerial Excellence

Be sensitive to people's feelings, and be kind to them.

Take time to make people feel special.

Listen to people's emotions as well as words.

View people's needs and wants as valid.

Choose your battles wisely.

Respect people's differences.

Avoid being defensive and placing people on the defensive.

Give people the benefit of the doubt.

Resolve interpersonal problems as quickly as possible,
    preferably before parting for any significant time.

In short, treat people the way you would like to be treated: as
    a valued friend.

Finally, never take people for granted—never.

Can you think of other, personal essentials for managerial excellence?

Genuine caring attitudes are key requirements for creating a fertile culture. The nature of attitudes, why they're important, and how you can develop attitudes that influence others to cooperate with you are the subjects of the next chapter.

Questions to Consider

- *What am I paid to do?*

- *What is my department's mission?*

- *What are some other essentials for managerial excellence in addition to the eleven listed?*

Positive attitudes lead to productive actions; negative attitudes lead to unproductive actions. Adopt and encourage positive attitudes.

One well-deserved, sincere, and specific compliment says more than a thousand insincere general ones.

Small acts of human kindness done consistently characterize a mensch.

2

Adopt Positive and Productive Attitudes

LET'S SAY YOU'VE BEEN INVITED TO a party to which you really don't want to go but for "politically correct" reasons you must attend. You don't have a choice of whether or not to accept the invitation, but you can choose your attitude regarding it.

By attitude, we mean a state of mind—an emotional and intellectual inclination—and a predisposition to actions based on what you tell yourself.

In the case of the party, if you were to choose a negative attitude, you would resent going. That's because you would tell yourself, "I really don't want to go to this party because I know I'll have a lousy time. I just know I will." Conversely, if you chose a positive attitude, you would feel OK about going, because you would tell yourself, "I really don't want to go to this party, but as long as I have to go, I will make every effort to have a good time."

In all likelihood, the attitude you chose would result in your prediction coming true. This phenomenon is called the self-fulfilling prophecy. It's almost like magic. When we have a strong belief about the outcome of a relationship or an impending experience, we do everything in our power to make that belief come true. It would not be an overstatement to say that our attitudes are responsible for creating, and even perpetuating, our joys and sorrows, our good and bad times, our successes and failures, and the quality of our relationships.

Since attitudes are powerful keys to your success as a manager, this chapter explains the nature of attitudes and how you can use positive attitudes to create a fertile departmental culture.

The Three Elements of Attitudes

The first element is what you tell yourself. As an activity, talking to yourself is neither good nor bad. We all do it. However, what you tell yourself can determine whether the consequences of your self-talk will be productive or unproductive.

The effect of self-talk on behavior is evident every day of our lives, both at work and at home. Consider the following example.

Several years ago, I was teaching a graduate class called Training and Development. One of the requirements was that each student teach the rest of the class to do something at which the presenter was competent.

About two weeks before one of my students, Marla, was due to conduct her teaching session, she came to me with a problem. "I get panicky whenever I have to make a presentation, either in class or at work," she said. "And because I get panicky, I always fail at this task. I don't want to fail anymore. I don't want to fail this class. What can I do to overcome my fear?"

I asked her what she tells herself just before making a presentation. "Nothing. I'm not aware of telling myself anything," she said.

"But you must," I insisted. "Think of the last time you had to make a presentation, and tell me about how you felt just before you had to do it."

She replied that a month ago she was required to present the results of a market research study she conducted to the company's advertising and sales departments. This report was to provide valuable insights for developing the company's marketing campaign. She said, "I was really nervous and was sure they would find fault with my conclusions. I thought they would make fun of my presentation. I was also scared they would ask me questions I wouldn't be able to answer."

After she relayed all of this negative self-talk, I asked her what happened. She said, "Most of my fears came true. My presentation was a flop. My presentations are always a flop. That's why I'm afraid of putting on a training session for the class."

What she had chosen for the assignment was to teach her fellow students to prepare an effective résumé. I asked, "Do you consider the skills you want to impart to the students important and valuable?"

"Yes, of course," she said.

"Then, this is what I want you to tell yourself a couple of days before your presentation: 'I am about to give this class a gift—one from which they will benefit. They will be better off for receiving this gift, and they will thank me for giving it to them. I am glad that I have the opportunity to share my knowledge with them.' "

An hour before her presentation, Marla came into my office to tell me how excited she was about the impending training session. "I really believe I'm about to give the class a gift they will cherish, and I'm looking forward to it. I wanted to come by to thank you," she said.

Marla's presentation was well received. She was poised, confident, and well organized. She focused on the information she was giving her students rather than on how they would receive her. Her actual performance, thus, was a clear example of a positive self-fulfilling prophecy.

The power of what people tell themselves is evident in another case, this one involving the customer service department of a former client, a medium-size manufacturing firm in the Midwest.

According to this client's vice president of operations, the company's customer service department was the object of frequent complaints. Specifically, people said they were treated rudely by customer service representatives, were left on hold for what seemed to be forever, were disconnected while waiting to be helped, and were not given the help they hoped to receive. These complaints, which were not offset by compliments, went on for about a year and were accompanied by a steady decline in sales.

When I met with the five-person department, I asked, "When the phone rings, what do you tell yourself before you answer it?" Every person related a variation of the same negative self-talk: "I wonder what this jerk wants" or "Oh, hell, here comes another complainer."

After discussing with the group the effect of self-talk on behaviors, I suggested that they tell themselves something else when the phone rings. For instance: "The caller has a problem, which is why he or she is phoning"; "My job of customer service representative is to help each caller with his or her problem"; "I am a valuable aid to people who are in trouble."

As part of the solution, they also adopted the greeting "How can I help you?" when answering the phone. This simple question was more than words. It was a genuine positive attitude, revealed in their tone of voice and helpful actions that said, in effect, "I care about your problem and have a sincere desire to help you."

Within a month, the vice president of operations started to receive calls from customers praising the customer service department's services.

The second element of attitude is your state of mind, which is engendered by thoughts and feelings resulting from what you tell yourself. *Attitude* is actually just another word for thoughts and feelings.

The third element is the actions stemming from a particular attitude.

The three elements are interdependent: What you tell yourself creates thoughts and feelings (attitudes) that lead to action. Therefore, to change your attitudes and actions, you must change what you tell yourself. The catch is to make sure you are sincere about what you tell yourself. If you're not, your self-talk will not engender the attitudes and actions you desire.

In general, positive attitudes, such as genuine caring or love, lead to helpful actions, whereas negative attitudes, such as unreasonable fear and anger, lead to defensive behaviors.

Following are three examples of how these elements work together when you give yourself positive messages.

Example 1

What you tell yourself: I am a student of everybody.

Possible attitudes: Inquisitive; curious; receptive to learning; respectful of "teachers."

Actions: Ask appropriate questions; listen attentively; express appreciation for the teacher's time and attention.

Example 2

What you tell yourself: I am a human being first, a manager second.

Possible attitudes: Caring and compassionate; sensitive; considerate and thoughtful.

Actions: Listen attentively; offer help when needed; be reasonably flexible.

Example 3

What you tell yourself: For every symptom there is a cause. If possible, don't treat symptoms, such as poor performance; determine the cause and then deal appropriately with the problem.

Possible attitudes: Viewing poor performance as a problem-solving challenge; probing for possible causes of the symptoms; making a commitment to finding a solution to the problem; challenging yourself to help the person find direction.

Actions: Ask appropriate questions; weigh alternative solutions to the problem; work with the employee to resolve the problem; encourage the employee to develop a positive attitude toward resolving the problem.

Discovery Lesson

To discover for yourself the relationship between what you tell yourself and what you do, complete this two-part exercise.

1. Come up with a negative statement about someone you know, using the person's name. Write this statement on a sheet of paper or in your manager's journal, and then read it aloud. Next, write down all the possible attitudes you could harbor toward this person that were triggered by the negative statement. Finally, write down all the actions that could result from your attitudes.

   Example: John is insensitive toward his fellow employees. He seems not to care when he puts someone on the spot publicly. When he is told what he does and the effect it has on people, he says, "They are overly sensitive."

   Attitudes I harbor toward John: No matter what I'd say or do, John would not pay attention to me. I really don't like John because he's disrupting my department. I can't trust John with projects that require him to work with others.

   Actions that could result from my negative attitudes toward John: I don't make a concerted effort to help John realize how he's affecting the department. I ignore John and allow others to follow my lead. I keep him isolated from the rest of the department.

2. Now come up with a positive statement about someone you know, again using the person's name. Follow the same procedure as you did in the first part of this exercise.

Example: Mary is conscientious and wants to succeed.

Attitudes I harbor toward Mary: She is a great addition to the department. Mary can be counted on to help anyone in the department who needs it. Because she's eager to learn, I want to help her in any way I can so she'll succeed. I'm eager to have her represent our department at major meetings with other departments.

Actions that result from my positive attitudes toward Mary: I include her in any project that could benefit from her expertise. I use her as a mentor for new employees requiring special attention. I go out of my way to teach her what I know.

What you should have discovered from this exercise is that positive attitudes lead to productive actions and negative attitudes lead to unproductive actions. To be a successful, professional manager, you'll want to encourage positive attitudes from all members of your department.

To reinforce a strong relationship among the three elements of attitude, do this: Every time you're feeling angry or hostile toward an employee, a customer, or anyone else who is important to you, ask yourself, "What am I telling myself that could be causing this negative reaction?" Once you've identified what you're telling yourself that's fostering this negativity, come up with a statement to yourself that could alter your state of mind.

For example, you might be angry with a particular employee for not doing what you asked. To change this negative thought, you should consider whether or not the employee was aware of your explicit expectations. Is it possible that you did not properly convey your expectations and have been operating under the erroneous assumption that your employee knew what was required of him? Since that is a possibility, you would simply ask your employee if you had told him what you expected from him. If properly phrased in a noncritical manner that doesn't make him feel as if he is under attack, your question should lead to an open dialogue with potential positive outcomes. These include better communication and understanding between your employee and yourself.

Or you might have someone in your department whom you consider to be a bad seed. Perhaps this person upsets the positive exchange of information within the group through defensiveness or a negative attitude. By merely observing that your employee is a bad seed, you do nothing to amend the situation. You need to take an active approach. Perhaps this person doesn't feel as if he or she fits in with the group. If this is the case, how might you encourage a sense of teamwork and cooperation?

Be more aware of your approach to interpersonal communications with your employees, and try replacing passive and negative thoughts with active and positive ones on a daily basis, and observe what happens.

Creating a Fertile Departmental Culture

To create and perpetuate a fertile departmental culture, you must encourage all employees to adopt attitudes that will enable them to be productive, to perform their jobs conscientiously, and to act professionally toward their coworkers, customers, vendors, and even competitors. You can do this by incorporating what we call the positive attitude adoption program. This program is a three-phase process that requires the cooperation and contributions of all your employees.

Phase 1

The objective of this phase is to compile a list of attitudes that reflect the values of your department. The two attitudes heading your list should be respectfulness and trustworthiness, which are the foundations of any meaningful relationship, be it personal or professional.

First you will need to call a departmental meeting. In advance of the meeting, tell your employees that in the interest of creating a fertile departmental culture that promotes employees' personal development and productivity, you are planning to initiate a positive attitude adoption program. You might want to define what an attitude is and then inform them that the two attitudes that will head your list are respectfulness and trustworthiness. Ask them to bring to the meeting a list of attitudes that they would like the department to adopt. At the meeting, discuss the attitudes presented by your employees, and agree on a final list.

Phase 2

At a follow-up meeting, for every attitude that you believe should be adopted, agree on how it could be converted into actions. Here is a composite list of "respectful" behaviors that were arrived at by several of our clients:

- Listen attentively without interruption, and make an effort to understand what is being said.
- Express gratitude when appropriate.

- Find value in any criticism you receive.
- Be polite.
- Ask for opinions, and seriously consider those opinions.
- Be considerate of each employee's feelings.
- Cooperate with each other because, even though we are a diverse community, we have common objectives.
- Celebrate each other's achievements, and extend sincere and specific compliments when appropriate.
- Return phone calls and E-mail messages as promptly as possible.
- Be forthright and compassionate in dealing with fellow employees.
- Extend yourself to fulfill customers' needs and their reasonable expectations.
- Have fun; enjoy what you do.

Feel free to include these behaviors when compiling your department's list. If you like, you can create several different lists of respectful behaviors. One list could comprise behaviors toward fellow employees, while another could emphasize behaviors toward customers, and still another might represent respectful behaviors that each individual should do for him- or herself. Included in this last list might be the following items: if something is worth doing, it's worth doing right and to the best of my ability; be attentive to details—that's the mark of a professional; and be kind to myself.

Your second list of positive departmental behaviors should demonstrate qualities of "trustworthiness." At the top of your department's list should be: Act responsibly—fulfill all promises, and don't make promises that the employee or department can't keep. Without this element of trustworthiness, the company's reputation among its clients and in the industry will be diminished.

Three other exemplary behaviors that appeared on many of our clients' lists were: maintain each other's confidence; do not judge each other's feelings; and be sincere.

Your list of trustworthy behaviors along with your lists of respectful behaviors will serve as a good start to achieve a positive departmental culture. As time permits, generate lists of behaviors that reflect the other attitudes you and your staff agreed to adopt.

Phase 3

In your final meeting in the series, decide as a group how you can reinforce the agreed-upon attitudes and the behaviors that reflect them. More specifically, how should employees respond when a coworker's behavior violates an attitude you agreed to adopt? One way is to be forthright and remind the offender that he or she agreed to abide by your departmental creed. However the reminder is expressed, it should be a gentle nudge and not a hit over the head with a two-by-four.

Being an excellent manager begins with being a good person— a mensch. A mensch is a respectful and genuine person who is sensitive and appropriately responsive to others' feelings. To qualify as a mensch, you must embody and consistently exhibit the following principles, attitudes, and behaviors in dealings with people:

- Be a perpetual student and learn from everyone, regardless of education, age, position, or status.
- In your desire to understand people, ask appropriate questions, in an appropriate way, at an appropriate time, and in an appropriate place.
- Act responsibly and kindly toward yourself and others.

- Listen attentively to what people say, both verbally and non-verbally, and respond appropriately to their messages.
- Demonstrate a genuine regard for all people's feelings, and accept those feelings as being valid.
- Be sensitively forthright and honest with people, leaving little to the fate of imagination and confusion.
- Don't allow defensiveness to dictate actions; all actions should be guided by a desire to be helpful and cooperative.
- Make people feel valued by asking for their opinions, requesting their help, praising commendable performance, and being polite and courteous at all times.

In short, by being considerate, righteous, and positive in all dealings with people, a mensch builds healthy communication bridges. By incorporating the qualities of a mensch into your managing style, you will foster excellent and positive communications and actions among your employees, your customers, and yourself.

In the Appendix, you'll find reproducible text highlighting the central points of this chapter which you may want to display in your workplace.

Questions to Consider

- *People who have positive attitudes tend to look at the whole. Those with negative attitudes do not see the W—they tend to focus on the hole. As a manager, one of your obligations is to teach your employees to add Ws in their lives. Do you agree? If so, how can you fulfill this obligation?*

- *Suppose you have a person in your department whose actions reflect a negative attitude. What specifically can you do to help this person alter his or her actions?*

- *Why does being an excellent manager begin with being a mensch?*

Knowledge is power. To increase your knowledge, welcome your employees' opinions, criticism, and questions.

Managing is an ongoing process of developing mutually rewarding relationships with your employees.

3

Get to Know Each Person in Your Department

PICTURE IN YOUR MIND'S EYE the best manager you've ever had. Now answer this question: On a scale of 1 to 10 (with 1 being the lowest), how well did this manager know and understand you? Assuming you gave the manager you envisioned an 8, 9, or 10, your rating is the same as that of most people to whom we've posed this question.

That shouldn't come as a surprise if you think about what managers actually communicate when they take the time to know and understand their employees. Speaking from our own experiences in working for such managers, these are some of the messages the persons' efforts communicated directly:

- I care about you as a person.
- You are important to me.
- I want to know how to talk to you and if there are any words I should avoid using because they offend you.
- I want to know how to motivate you to be the best you can be.
- I want to know your vocational aspirations.
- I want to know what you want from life, besides being vocationally successful.
- I want to know what's important to you and what isn't.
- I want to know what specifically you expect from me as your manager.

Because those messages made the employees in the department feel valued, we did everything in our power to extend ourselves for these managers. Wouldn't you, if you felt valued? Wanting to do your best for someone who respects you and is interested in you as a person is a natural human reaction. It is how your employees will respond to you if you convey to them these positive messages.

A friend recently forwarded an E-mail memo that supports this theme of human reactions and feelings. It related how a flight attendant resolved a passenger's problem with a thoughtful goodwill gesture that made the passenger feel special. At the end of the story, the originator of the memo wrote: "People may forget what you said; they may even forget what you did; but rarely, if ever, will they forget how you made them feel." (You'll find this quote reproduced in the Appendix.)

How do you want your employees to feel? Do you want them to feel special? Do you want them to feel that you genuinely care about them as people as well as producers? Do you want them to feel important? Do you want them to feel respected? Do you want them to feel trusted? Your answer to all these questions is probably, "Of course I do."

The most effective first step for creating these feelings in your employees is to take time to get to know them. Learn about their interests, their likes, their dislikes, their vulnerabilities, their hopes and dreams, their vocational aspirations, their pet peeves, and all the other characteristics that define them as the individuals they are. You should view your efforts to learn about them as a worthy investment of your time and effort, because by creating a sense of familiarity and camaraderie, you will increase employee motivation and loyalty.

Another friend, a member of a local garden club, was an expert on growing prize-winning orchids; his plants won first or second place in every horticultural contest he entered. When asked the secret of his many horticultural successes, he said that he learned from books and other orchid growers precisely what these special plants needed from him to thrive, and then he created the atmosphere that enabled them to do just that. Thus, it's simple to grow orchids when you provide them with what they need and check up on them to make sure the conditions are consistent with their requirements.

Share a Table for Two

When you get to know the people who report to you, you will form bonds that make it easier to communicate with them, to resolve differences, and to solve mutual problems. Those benefits will pay great dividends for both you and them.

The process of getting to know your employees is not difficult. It begins with a genuine desire to learn all you can about each member of your staff and an interest in finding the best way of doing that. One way is to make individual lunch dates with each of your employees. This is not a one-time investment but an ongoing process that will put you in personal contact several times with each employee over the course of a few months. Initially, you may want to schedule lunch with each employee every other week. Later, you may limit the meetings to coffee breaks.

At a departmental meeting, simply tell your employees that you are interested in getting to know each of them and that you want them, in turn, to get to know you. Inform them that you will be meeting with everyone in the department, so that no one will feel singled out, and that the atmosphere will be informal, so that they do not feel anxious about the occasion. Let them know that you will both agree on a schedule well in advance, so that they can plan accordingly, and that you are looking forward to these meetings, which should be both fun and interesting. At the end of your announcement, be sure to ask if anyone has any questions. Employees may well have concerns about the content of the meetings. They may wonder if you have a particular agenda in mind, since it is, sadly, rare that managers make such concerted efforts to get to know their staffs.

"Get to Know You" Questions

When meeting individually with your employees, remember that your objectives are to get to know your staff and to give them the opportunity to get to know you. You can accomplish this by asking direct questions, as you would in an interview, or by posing a problem or two—preferably real ones—and asking your luncheon companion how he or she would deal with each one. You could also combine the two formats. However you proceed, your approach should not be intimidating.

To set the stage for positive communication, make sure to tell your employees beforehand that you want to discuss ways to improve their work environment, their job satisfaction, and your abilities as a manager. Do your best to create a relaxed, casual environment conducive to open dialogue and laughter.

Following are a few of the questions you may want to ask, although not necessarily in the form they are given. Always approach your interactions with your employees in a way that is natural to you. Disregard any questions with which you are uncomfortable, and, by all means, generate meaningful questions of your own.

- When you think about going to work, what do you look forward to doing? What excites and challenges you in your job?
- What, if anything, do you dread when you think about going to work?
- If you had a magic wand, what specifically would you change in our department? Why? What difference would that change make?
- I want to be the best manager I can be for you. What do you want me to know about you that would help me do that?
- What specifically do you need from me as your manager? (Then, proceed to discuss each need in detail.)
- Will you describe for me the worst manager you ever had? What kinds of things did this manager do that made him or her the worst?
- Will you describe for me the best manager you ever had? What kinds of things did this manager do that made him or her the best?

Strategy for Asking Questions

Discussions of each one of the questions listed could take the better part of a lunch hour. For example, if you were to ask the last question, follow-up questions to the employee's initial response might be: How did specific things the manager did or said make you feel? Will you give me an example of how this manager handled problems that arose in the department? Were there certain qualities about this person that you liked? What were they?

Initial responses to each of these questions can stimulate more questions whose answers could, in turn, stimulate additional ones. Such in-depth discussions tell you a great deal about a person. Even if you delve into only one or two questions per meeting, as long as the discussion is informative and helps you know and understand the employee better than you did before, you have accomplished your goal.

Do not follow the same routine with each employee, to avoid giving the impression that each interview is identical. Instead, apply the concept of planned spontaneity. This means that you know in advance what you hope to gain from the meeting, you know where you want to begin (making sure you don't start off with the same question with each employee), and you allow the answer to each question to determine where you go with it. Planned spontaneity can lead you to beneficial discoveries and pleasant surprises. All you need to do is listen intently and ask appropriate questions. (The dos and don'ts of asking questions are the subject of Chapter 11.) You may find that you spent the entire lunch hour examining only one of the questions you hoped to discuss. That's fine as long as you learned something valuable about your employee and vice versa.

Discovery Lesson

This exercise is similar to the one for creating a positive attitude adoption program in Chapter 2.

On a page of your journal, list as many qualities as you can think of that you would like your employees to feel (e.g., respected, trusted, appreciated, important).

On a separate page, for each feeling you listed, write down your answer to this question: What specifically do I need to do to foster this feeling? Refer to this list of desirable behaviors as often as necessary throughout the course of your managerial career.

Questions to Consider

- *What other questions might I ask my employees during our lunches?*

After meeting with employees:

- *What value did I gain from conducting my interviews?*

- *Specifically, how can I use the knowledge I gained to help my employees be as productive as they can be?*

People who give of themselves to others also give to themselves.

4

What You and Your Employees Have in Common

YOU ARE A HUMAN BEING FIRST and a manager second. Since your employees are also human beings first, you already have much in common with them. This means that your employees' expectations of you are not that much different from your expectations of your own manager or of your managers in the past. Likewise, your employees' desires of you (which are more than expectations) are not much different from the desires you have of your manager.

This realization should motivate you to treat your employees the way you would like to be treated. Of course, you hold a position of greater responsibility, but the characteristics you have in common with your employees—your human characteristics—are far more significant than your differences, such as your respective job titles, sex, race, or religion.

To sharpen your sense of how much you and the people under your influence have in common, complete the following three-part discovery exercise.

Discovery Lesson

1. On a sheet of paper, write your answer to this question: What, specifically, do I expect from my manager or the person to whom I report?

   Expectations in this context refer to all entitlements and anything and any treatment you consider essential to performing your job. For example, it is reasonable for you to expect a safe workplace, a clear understanding of what is required of you, and respect. These are basic essentials.

   If these and other minimal expectations were unfulfilled, you would be disappointed, unhappy, and probably inclined to look for other employment. Yet, even if your minimal expectations were fulfilled, you would not be jumping up and down with excitement. More to the point, you would not be motivated to do your best; most likely, you would simply do whatever it takes to get by. This is because it's normal for employees to give no more than they receive. That's the way it is with all perceived entitlements: it's no big deal to receive what you believe you have coming to you.

2. On a separate sheet of paper, answer this question: What, specifically, do I desire from my manager?

This list will be different from your list of expectations. Desires, when fulfilled, are like unexpected bonuses or other pleasant surprises. We call them "It sure would be nice if _____" things. Some examples of desires are recognition for achievements that exceed your manager's expectations, challenges that recognize your skills, requests for your opinion, and any creative ways of making you feel valued. Typically, when desires are fulfilled, employees extend themselves and perform above and beyond what's expected of them.

3. Review each of the two lists you just created, and answer this question: If my employees listed these same expectations and desires, how would I rate as a manager in fulfilling them consistently?

    If you hold certain expectations and desires of your manager, doesn't it stand to reason that your employees hold similar expectations and desires of you? Examine your notes and see for yourself if you are fulfilling your employees' possible expectations and desires.

Previous chapters discussed ways in which you can develop a mutual trusting relationship with your employees. If you have accomplished this task, we salute you! You are on your way to becoming a successful manager. If not, you have missed an integral step in the managing process, so please go back and examine ways to build such a relationship. Once you have done so, continue to strengthen your relationships with your employees throughout the course of your career as a manager.

In order to open the lines of communication between you and your employees, you need to elicit exactly what it is that they expect and desire of you. As noted in the Discovery Lesson, in many cases, their answers will not be much different from your own expectations and desires of your manager. However, each job and each employee carries a unique set of wants and desires, and it is to your benefit to find out what these are. The following is one way to do this, but you may choose a method of your own that produces the same positive results and communication.

Send a memo to each of your employees requesting their comments on how you can improve upon your performance as a manager. If you have only a few employees, you may want to talk with them directly instead. For example:

> Memo: I want to be the best manager I can be for you. To do that, I'm enlisting your help. Please respond to the following four items and give your responses to me within the week. Be completely honest—I'm trying to improve my performance as your manager, and your assistance is much needed and much appreciated.
>
> 1. Tell me specifically all the things you *expect* from me as your manager.
> 2. Concerning each of your expectations listed above, how effectively and consistently, on a scale of 1 (low) to 10, do I fulfill it?
> 3. Complete the following sentence concerning your *desires* in as many ways as you would like: Although I don't expect it, it sure would be nice if you _____.
> 4. Concerning each of the desires you mentioned in question 3, rate how important each is to you: 1 (very important), 2 (important), or 3 (slightly important).
>
> Please put your name on the paper and, in the spirit of helpfulness, feel free to add any other comments.

When drafting your memo, be conscious of the language you use. You want your employees to feel comfortable offering constructive criticism. Assure them that their responses will not detrimentally affect them or your treatment of them in the workplace.

Seriously evaluate the information and comments that your employees give you, with the knowledge that how effectively you motivate and manage people determines your managerial success. To fully benefit from what you learn, in your manager's journal make note of all of the expectations and desires that were expressed. You may find comments that occur repeatedly, in one way or another, from different employees; pay particular attention to these. Next, determine specific ways in which you can fulfill these desires and expectations. Record specific actions and solutions in your journal for future reference.

Taking a proactive stance in improving your managerial capabilities will prove beneficial to your happiness and success as a manager and to the happiness and success of your department as a whole.

Questions to Consider

- *What do my employees expect from me? How do I plan to fulfill their reasonable expectations?*

- *What desires do my employees have of me? How do I plan to fulfill those that are reasonable?*

- *What benefits do I anticipate from answering the preceding questions?*

If you want to understand management, read books and go to classes that teach it. If you want to know how to manage your employees, go to them and listen to what they say.

Every action or reaction communicates something. By determining what each something is, you become more enlightened.

5

Listen—Really Listen— and You Will Hear More than Words

WHAT IS THE MESSAGE CONVEYED BY the title of this chapter? How do we distinguish between listening and *really* listening? The following anecdote illustrates the difference between the two and how, if you care enough to try, you can hear "more than words."

A well-known symphony conductor was holding auditions for a new pianist for his orchestra. One particular candidate came highly recommended, and many supporters were sure he would be selected because of his mastery and technique at the keyboard. The candidate played flawlessly at the audition, to the surprise of no one. However, he was not selected. The disappointed supporters asked the conductor why he declined to hire this pianist, who had played the composition perfectly. The maestro said, "Your protégé did play perfectly. He played all the notes exactly as they were written. That's important, of course, but we need much more: we are looking for someone who will play the music." Everyone understood the decision instantly. Precision is substantially different from passion.

When you listen to your employees, you must listen for the music, not just the notes. Listen for the feelings, not just the facts. Listen not only to what is said but also to the way it is said. In short, listen to the tone of the words your employees use as well as to the words themselves.

What Tone Can Tell You

Tone relates to the emphasis given to specific words, to the speed of the delivery, to the volume, and to the pitch of the voice. They all modify the words. To demonstrate, read this sentence aloud: I can't believe he stole that money.

Now change the emphasis of the individual words as indicated:

I can't believe he stole that money.
I **can't** believe he stole that money.
I can't **believe** he stole that money.
I can't believe **he** stole that money.

I can't believe he **stole** that money.

I can't believe he stole **that** money.

I can't believe he stole that **money**.

Notice how the meaning changes? The notes are the same, but the music is different.

How do you and your employees talk to each other? Are your tones supportive, intimidating, aggressive, confrontational, friendly, or something else? Listen for the tone in what your employees say in order to determine the mood and motivation behind each statement.

In the police drama "Dragnet," Jack Webb as the no-nonsense detective Joe Friday often recited the line "Just the facts, Ma'am." It worked for him in the program because that's how the script was written, and he knew the ending. However, since you are working without a script, and you cannot presume to know what your employees are thinking, the facts aren't enough. You need to sense the feelings and motivations behind the words. And remember, for every one of us, it's the feelings, the emotions, that drive our behavior.

How do your employees feel about you and about each other? How do they feel about their jobs? About what you ask them to do? About your methods of handling problems? If you listen—really listen—you'll detect the clues that will help you answer these questions. You'll sense the motives and the passion behind your employees' actions. And that's what forms a bond, a relationship. If you don't listen carefully and attentively, you'll create a distance between yourself and your employees because you will not hear what they are trying to tell you through more subtle forms of communication.

Discovery Lesson

Walk through your department and pay close attention to what is going on around you. Listen carefully to the words you overhear, and think about what the words really mean, what meaning a certain tone of voice is conveying, and which particular words have the potential to set off or cool down a conflict. If employees speak differently to different coworkers, try to determine the precise difference and what might account for it.

Applying what you learn from listening to your employees will help you better deliver your messages and ideas to them. By increasing your sensitivity toward your employees, by learning what turns them off and what turns them on, and by identifying the interpersonal dynamics of the members of your staff, you will become keenly aware of the most positive and productive ways to promote communication. Because communication is a two-way street, you need to be sure the "traffic" flows both ways.

Building a Communication Bridge

As a manager, you must create a communication bridge between you and the people who report to you. The purpose of this bridge is for you to connect with each of your employees and for them to connect with you. If you convey the attitude that you care enough about your employees to really listen to them, you can solidify a two-way connection that is mutually rewarding.

Unfortunately, building such a bridge is easier said than done. The problem is that people communicate all the time on three levels: by what they say, by how they say it, and by what they do when they say it.

Let's be clear about what is meant by communication: anything, verbal or nonverbal, that imparts information, thoughts, or feelings. Effective communication between you and your employees occurs when your intended messages and their received messages are essentially the same, and vice versa.

For example, suppose you call an employee's attention to a weakness and then suggest how it can be corrected. If the person receives your message (your constructive criticism) as a gift, your communication is effective. If instead the employee reacts defensively and reads your comment as an attack, your communication is not effective and, therefore, must be modified.

Likewise, for you to accurately receive the intended verbal messages of your employees, you must be a sensitive listener. This means being fully engaged; your brain, ears, eyes, heart, and soul must be involved. You can best accomplish this state by adopting the following attitude: The person talking to me is the most important person in my life at this moment.

To genuinely exhibit this attitude, concentrate on the person talking to you, and don't allow yourself to be distracted. If you don't have time to give an employee your undivided attention, explain the situation and schedule a time when you will be available. It will not do your employee, your organization, or you any good to lend only half an ear.

Discovery Lesson

Again recall the best manager you ever had. Think back to a time when you came to this manager with a concern that you needed to have resolved. How did this person make you feel during your conversation? What specifically did the manager do to create that feeling? Record your observations in your manager's journal, and keep the lesson as a reminder of what you might do to sharpen your listening skills.

Conversely, think again of the worst manager you ever had, and examine the way this person approached your concerns. Do you find yourself exhibiting any of these characteristics? Have you in the past? If so, what steps can you take to change these behaviors? How can you approach issues differently?

Detecting Hidden Messages

When listening to employees, bear in mind that most messages have three parts to them, as noted in the previous section. (1) The verbal part of the message is revealed by what is actually said. (2) The emotional part is revealed by how it is said; that is, the tone of voice and the words that are emphasized. (3) The nonverbal part is revealed by what is done while it is being said, or even afterward. Listen for harmony or dissonance: Do the tone of the message and the actions that accompany it reflect the words that were used?

See if you can tell what is actually being communicated in the following messages from employees to their managers. The words are clear, but what other messages are there?

- Don't you think we have too many meetings?
- You're in charge; I'll do it the way you want.
- Why is it every time we make an appointment to get together, the meeting gets canceled?
- What do I have to do to gain some appreciation around here?
- I don't know whether you realize it, but the only time I hear from you is when I screw up in some way.

If you're really listening, you'll hear the hidden message in each of these remarks, as well as others you may encounter daily, and acknowledge them. When you do hear such comments from your employees, ask the speakers what they really mean and if they can suggest some ways to make positive changes. An acknowledgment says, in effect, "I hear what you're really saying, and I invite you to elaborate."

In response to the first question, for example, you would acknowledge the hidden message by asking if the employee felt there were too many departmental meetings, if he or she felt some of these meetings were unproductive, and what might be done to improve the situation.

Your acknowledgment in turn conveys at least three messages to your employee. First, it recognizes that the employee isn't categorically objecting to the meetings but believes that their content and productivity don't necessitate as many meetings as are actually held. Second, it reflects your understanding that the employee wants to be asked what prompted the comment. And third, it affirms that you care enough about what the employee thinks to ask for his or her opinions on how to make the department more productive.

In the second statement cited—You're in charge; I'll do it the way you want—the hidden message may be that the speaker doesn't approve of the method or process of a particular activity. The employee may be too shy to offer his or her opinion and is instead inviting you to solicit it. By acknowledging the underlying message and asking how the speaker might conduct the process differently, you convey that you are sensitive to the person's thoughts and insights and that you consider the person a valuable member of your department. As you can see, you must be a sensitive listener in order to decipher underlying emotional messages; you have to hear more than the words.

Let's analyze the remaining three statements on the list to discover what emotional undercurrents reside in them.

Statement: Why is it every time we make an appointment to get together, the meeting gets canceled? *Emotional undercurrent:* The employee is frustrated and feels undervalued and unimportant. The employee wants your undivided attention and feels entitled to it. *Acknowledgment:* Instead of countering with the reasons why you have had to cancel each of your previously scheduled meetings, inform the speaker that you recognize the underlying message. Affirm that the employee is a valuable addition to your team and that, in the future, you will strive to keep your appointments without interruptions. Back up this promise with action.

Statement: What do I have to do to gain some appreciation around here? *Emotional undercurrent:* The speaker feels taken for granted and believes that his or her hard work and successful efforts are not properly credited. Not feeling valued has made the employee angry. *Acknowledgment:* State that you do indeed value the person and the person's contributions to your department. Reinforce this statement with private and public commendations of the employee's performance. Ask what actions on your part might make the employee feel more appreciated.

The final statement is a variation of the previous one and carries a similar hidden message: I don't know whether you realize it, but the only time I hear from you is when I screw up in some way. Your acknowledgment, likewise, will be a variation of the previous one.

In summary, acknowledgments of your employees' hidden messages convey your interest in them as people, your sensitivity, and your sincere desire to be the best manager you can be. This attitude will help you find the correct words to acknowledge your employees' emotions. Remember that under no circumstances is it appropriate to judge emotions. If you convey to your employees that their feelings are unwarranted and inappropriate, you will create a negative, divisive atmosphere. Similarly, if you make employees feel insulted, you are likely to precipitate defensive reactions that will negatively affect their productivity and your departmental culture.

You will accomplish three important goals by acknowledging and not judging your employees' emotions. First, your employees will feel that they can trust you and that you care. Second, employees' trust in you will encourage two-way communication. And third, you will assure your employees that they are on a cooperative team.

To underscore the difference between the responses of someone who really listens and one who doesn't, go back to each of the five statements and respond to the verbal part of the message only. By disregarding the underlying messages and responding to only the words, you are announcing that you are insensitive to the speakers' feelings and that you aren't interested in hearing what they really have to say. Obviously, such responses discourage effective communication.

A manager named Mitch shared this anecdote about how responding to only the verbal part of a message proved costly to him. Mitch had an employee, Bill, whom he greatly valued and for whom he would do just about anything to ensure his loyalty. In an effort to do just that, Mitch would ask him at least once a week, "How are things going, Bill?" Bill, not being much of a talker, would always say, "Fine" or "Very well, thank you."

One week, in response to the same question, Bill said, "OK, I guess." Although this response should have been acknowledged, Mitch wasn't sensitive to the fact that this answer was markedly different from Bill's usual replies. Thus, Mitch assumed that everything was just fine with Bill. After all, that's what the words communicated. You can imagine Mitch's surprise when, after a couple of weeks of this exchange, Bill announced his resignation because he had found another position more to his liking.

A simple acknowledgment—"What do you mean by you 'guess'? Is something wrong?" or "Sounds as if something's bothering you; let's get together to talk about it."—would have given Mitch a chance to resolve Bill's concerns.

Principles and Guidelines for Acknowledging Nonverbal Communication

Your employees frequently express their thoughts and feelings by what they do or don't do. Since those nonverbal actions and reactions are often more powerful than words, they must be acknowledged, just as emotions expressed through words must be acknowledged. Under no circumstances should they be ignored. The principles and guidelines that follow, as well as the examples of how to acknowledge both negative and positive actions, will provide you with the tools you need to develop healthy relationships with your employees.

Principle 1

Any negative behavior that deviates from a person's normal actions should be acknowledged.

The objectives of this acknowledgment are to determine the causes of the deviation and to solve the problem. An acknowledgment of a negative behavior says, in effect, "I sense that something is not quite right with you, and I'd like to know what it is so we can correct it and move forward."

For example, Anna has been a model employee from the time you hired her. Her disposition is always positive, and her performance has always met your highest standards. However, about a week ago, you noticed a change. She is short with everyone in the department, and the quality of her work has declined substantially. Essentially, she has not been herself lately. How do you acknowledge what you see?

You might start by pulling Anna aside and telling her that you have noted a change in her behavior. Inform her that this concerns you because she has always been a happy and productive worker, and ask if there is anything she would like to tell you. Make sure the words you choose and your tone of voice are reassuring and nonconfrontational. In so doing you would clearly communicate a caring attitude and a desire to help resolve the problem expressed nonverbally by the employee.

Principle 2

Positive behaviors, particularly those that exceed your normal expectations, should also be acknowledged.

Acknowledgments of positive behaviors say, in effect, "I value your work, and I do not take you for granted." The more specific you can be, the more effective the acknowledgment.

For example, Zack could best be described as a star employee. He typically is the first person in the office and usually stays after normal hours. It's not just a matter of putting in time that makes him valuable to the department but also his attitude toward his responsibilities, which is, in essence, "Good enough is not good enough for me; I want my work to reflect my high standards and best efforts." Furthermore, he readily volunteers to help coworkers when they have a problem. In all, he is an outstanding asset to the department.

Should those conscientious efforts be taken for granted? Of course not! If you do so, you risk losing a valuable employee. An appropriate acknowledgment, in the privacy of your office, of your employee's conscientious contributions to your department would be a simple and effective means of building employee loyalty. An additional acknowledgment might be to take the employee out to lunch to show him your appreciation for his contributions above and beyond the call of duty. Saying thank you and expressing your appreciation of employees' efforts will go a long way in building a satisfied and productive workforce.

Principle 3

Whether you are acknowledging negative or positive nonverbal behavior, the primary attitude that must come through is: "I genuinely care about you as a person as well as in your role as a productive member of our department."

All of us like to feel that we are appreciated for who we are as well as for what we do. We communicate who we are by our facial expressions and physical demeanor, but it is not always clear to others what is going on inside. If you sense negative nonverbal behavior, a simple comment, such as "I sense that something is bothering you" or "Looks as if you're having a tough day," is an acknowledgment that might get the employee talking. If, on the other hand, you sense a positive nonverbal behavior, a comment such as "You look as if you just won the lottery; you want to tell me what's causing you to look and sound so great?" would convey a caring attitude.

Listening to Nonverbal Messages

In the following situations, the nonverbal messages speak volumes. After you read each setup, apply the guidelines and principles presented in this chapter to answer these questions: What do you hear this employee telling you? How would you effectively acknowledge the nonverbal message?

Sara is an employee who, until recently, had been performing admirably for as long as you've known her. In the past few days, however, you've noticed a significant decline in both the quality and quantity of her work. Also, during the past two weeks she has been coming in late and leaving exactly when she's supposed to.

You recently hired Jonah under the assumption that he would fit in with your department. Since his experience was consistent with what you needed, you thought he would require no training to do his job. Now, three weeks after Jonah began work, one of your senior employees calls your attention to the fact that this new employee has been making an inordinate number of errors. Since Jonah hasn't been coming to you for help, you assumed that he knew what he was doing. Except for the errors, there have been no symptoms of other problems.

Roberto is an employee who is dependable and conscientious in every way, but he is extremely quiet. In departmental meetings, he does not say a word. This bothers you because you know his contributions could benefit the department, but you've been reluctant to say anything to him about it because you don't want him to think you're adversely judging him.

The purpose of the next Discovery Lesson is to increase your confidence in your ability to "listen to behaviors." If you want to be an excellent listener, you must always tune in to all the messages directly conveyed to you as well as those you observe and sense. Verbal, emotional, and behavioral messages all fit together. When any one isn't present, the communication may be incomplete. It's up to you to determine what's missing and then take steps to complete the communication, either by asking questions or by making additional observation.

Discovery Lesson

Listed here are a few common emotions or attitudes expressed in work situations. For each one, describe in your manager's journal the nonverbal behaviors you might observe that would indicate these feelings. One or two examples for each are provided to get you started.

Fear: When asked for an opinion on an issue, the employee declines to express it or says, "I don't have an opinion." Fear may also be the cause of employees' reluctance to say what is on their minds.

Anger: An employee raises his or her voice or yells at the slightest provocation. An employee is highly judgmental of other departmental members.

Unhappiness: An employee walks around with a sour face or frequently complains.

Boredom or feeling unchallenged: Procrastination is often a symptom, as is a lack of enthusiasm for assignments.

Conscientiousness: The employee usually does more than is required. The employee sets high standards, and his or her performance consistently reflects those standards.

Caring: The employee takes a sincere interest in others and asks appropriate questions that reflect this attitude.

Respect for fellow employees: The employee is considerate of people's needs and listens attentively to others.

Upbeat and positive in approach to life and work: The employee has a good sense of humor and looks at the brighter side of life.

Throughout your managerial career, keep in mind that every action communicates something. To be an effective manager, you have to make a conscious effort to determine the message communicated by each action.

Remember that you need to hear more than the notes; you need to hear the music.

Questions to Consider

- *Why do you think poor listening is the single biggest problem in business? What are the possible consequences wherever that problem exists?*

- *What specifically are you willing to do to improve your listening skills?*

- *What do you anticipate will be the positive outcomes of improving your listening skills?*

- *Specifically, how can you promote good listening skills in your department?*

If at first you don't succeed, determine what went wrong, make appropriate changes, and then try again.

Don't allow employees to use you as an excuse for not fulfilling their commitments. Give them whatever they need that's reasonable so they can fulfill their commitments.

Don't use anyone as an excuse for not moving forward. Obtain from people whatever you need to excel.

6

Perpetuate Problem–Solving Attitudes

MANAGING IS AN ONGOING PROCESS of developing mutually rewarding relationships between you and your employees. Previous chapters presented skills and techniques you can use to develop these positive relationships. By adopting attitudes that produce a positive working environment, getting to know each person in your department, recognizing the characteristics you have in common with your employees, and really listening to them, you will set an example and set the stage for a positive, productive working environment.

You can also bring positive problem-solving skills and attitudes to your department in order to further this goal. You and your employees will accomplish much by committing yourselves to helping each other solve your respective problems.

In this context, a problem constitutes a deviation between a reasonable want—that is, what is acceptable to you—and what actually is occurring.

To prove the practical validity of this explanation, recall two or three major problems you have encountered recently at work. Concerning each problem, answer the following two questions: What made it a problem? What did you want that you lacked? Almost always, your answer to both questions will be essentially the same.

Moving from Negative to Positive

Each of the examples in this section contains a description of the implied deviation between what you as manager expect or want and what you're actually getting, and one or two questions that, when answered, should lead to a reasonable outcome.

- You have an employee whose contributions to your department are substantially less than what she is capable of giving. Why is she not fulfilling her potential? What courses of action are available to help her and you resolve this problem?
- You have two employees who must work together, but they don't like each other and would rather not be teamed. Furthermore, their mutual dislike is adversely affecting their per-

formance. How can you help them foster more positive attitudes toward each other that will lead to mutual cooperation and respect?

- One of your employees is overly sensitive and becomes defensive when you or other members of the department correct him or attempt to help him. What can you do to make him realize that he needs to be more receptive to help?
- You have an employee who doesn't have a positive thing to say about anything. Worse, she is constantly complaining about something. For her, the glass is almost always half empty, and when she looks at a doughnut, she sees only the hole. What are the reasons for this negativity? Are there ways of getting this employee to view things differently?
- You have an employee who, for as long as you've known him, has been upbeat and highly motivated. Recently, you've noticed a negative change in his demeanor and a decline in his performance. Why the sudden change? What can you do to help him resolve his concerns?

These are all situations you may encounter, and doubtless there will be many others. Regardless of the predicament you confront, to effect resolution, always state it, to yourself or to your employees, in positive terms. Compare, for example, the following two statements: (1) "My problem is that Joe's performance for the past month has been deteriorating." (2) "I need to find out why Joe's performance has deteriorated during the last month so we can arrive at some ways to help him improve." The first statement is nothing more than a complaint. The second, which portrays the case in positive terms, acknowledges that something is causing the decline in performance and that you're interested in helping the person remedy the problem you've described.

Now compare these two statements: (1) "My problem is that our department is under great pressure." (2) "My problem is that our department is under great pressure, and it's my job to figure out what's causing it and what we can do to alleviate the situation." Again, the first rendering is a complaint, or a negative/passive statement; the second one is concerned with resolution, or a positive/active statement.

Whenever employees come to you with problems stated in negative terms, as a complaint, you could help by raising two proactive, positive questions: what they specifically want or need that they do not currently have, and what actions they can take to solve the problem with or without your assistance. These proactive questions will stimulate problem-solving attitudes and reinforce corresponding problem-solving skills among your employees.

Initially, you know you have a problem when you observe symptoms—deviations from normality—that bother you. Symptoms are anything that tell you something is not quite right or is not the way you want it to be. For example, symptoms of an unhealthy plant include drooping leaves, leaves turning yellow, and edges of leaves turning brown. Similarly, when you have a low-grade fever and a runny nose and are inordinately tired or unusually irritable, you are exhibiting symptoms of a common cold or perhaps something more complicated. Being aware of symptoms and having a keen ability to recognize them is important because they are red flags that signal either an impending problem or the early stages of an existing problem.

Acknowledging that you have a problem in your department or with an employee, or that you are on the verge of encountering one, is a prerequisite to solving it. However, the difficulty you're experiencing will continue, and may even get worse, until you take the next step, which is to ask yourself, "What am I going to do to resolve my problem?"

A fact you must accept is this: Every problem you have is your responsibility. If, for instance, you were the manager of a department in which any of the five situations listed at the beginning of the chapter existed, it would be your problem, even though you can identify a particular employee who is causing it. It would be your problem because the symptom you're seeing is a deviation from your desires and expectations of your department. Therefore, you must take responsibility for solving it as well as any other problems that arise in your department.

How you tackle your problems tells your employees what kind of person you are, what type of departmental culture you want to cultivate, and what you expect of them in similar situations. Since your employees likely will follow your lead, you have the power to create either a defensive culture or a problem-solving culture. To help you exercise your power wisely, the following sections examine and compare the characteristics of each.

Characteristics of a Defensive Culture

The dominant and pervasive attitude of employees in a defensive culture is paralyzing fear—fear of expressing opinions, taking risks, being adversely judged, being misunderstood, being wrongly penalized, and doing or saying anything they feel might threaten their position or image. Because employees are fearful, their number one objective is to protect themselves from getting emotionally hurt and from tarnishing their image, which they believe is positive.

Sometimes, to make themselves look good, employees will undermine and find fault with others. Worse, they harbor variations of such attitudes as "Every man for himself," "It's a dog-eat-dog world," and "I do what's best for me." The result of these negative mind-sets is that *I* takes precedence over *we*. Since a department is by definition a collective group of individuals, this negative mind-set does nothing to maintain or advance the productivity of the group and is inevitably detrimental to your department.

Many of the conversations in defensive cultures are personal and tainted with accusatory language such as "You are . . . ," "You don't . . . ," "You never . . . ," and "You always . . . " followed by negative phrases that can put people on the defensive. Blaming, finding fault, making excuses, close-mindedness, dishonesty, hold-ing grudges, jealousies, and spreading negative rumors are also prevalent. These are not necessarily signs of bad apples in your department, but they are all unhealthy expressions of insecurity and trepidation.

Managers and other employees in such cultures are so caught up with their inordinate need to be right and to look good that they fail to see the consequences of their egocentric and defensive atti-tudes. In reality, these attitudes are like weeds, which rob gardens of vital nutrients. A weed-infested department stifles creativity, dis-courages innovative thinking, and stunts the growth and the devel-opment of its employees.

How Negative Influence Is Spread

How do potentially good managers create such a bad culture? Obvi-ously, it's not intentional. No manager we know starts the morning saying, "I wonder what I can do today to create a defensive depart-ment." Nor does any manager we know say, "What can I do to cause my employees to be afraid of me and of each other?" Never-theless, their words and actions do both. Following are several com-mon ways in which managers of defensive cultures spread their negative influence.

They are judgmental and engage in personal assassinations. Judgments essentially say, implicitly or explicitly, "You don't know what you're talking about," "Your opinions and beliefs are not worthy of consideration," "Your attitude is terrible," or even "You're a fool." Personal assassinations typically begin with "You" or "Your," followed by a negative comment. By making such a pat statement about an individual, managers are being judgmental.

They believe they have all the answers and do not value their employees' contributions. The actions of these defensive managers, as well as their words, communicate the attitude "If you don't see things the same way I do, there is something wrong with you" or "I have all the answers." Managers who convey these attitudes stifle give-and-take between themselves and their employees. They also discourage employees from contributing their knowledge and experience.

They make employees feel guilty for making mistakes. We all make mistakes, and as long as we learn from them and do not repeat them, we benefit from the experience. Managers who undermine their employees for being human communicate a message that it's wrong and it's bad to err. This message causes employees to be afraid to take risks, even reasonable ones. Since all progress requires a certain amount of risk, instilling a fear of taking risks and of making mistakes is tantamount to preventing employees from growing.

They make employees feel stupid for asking questions. An old saying tells us that there are no stupid questions. In fact, if you want to know the answer to a question, it's stupid *not* to ask. By discouraging employees from asking questions, whether this is stated or conveyed through negative reactions to questions, a manager fails in one of the job's main functions: to be a teacher. In making employees feel uncomfortable asking questions, these managers are inadvertently hurting the department and the people in it. Excellent managers encourage their employees to ask questions when they are unclear about anything.

They dignify defensiveness by allowing an employee to blame others for failing to fulfill his or her own responsibilities, by accepting excuses as substitutes for facts, or by condoning behaviors that do not serve the best interests of the department. Actions that do not lead a person at least one step closer to meeting reasonable objectives are ineffective. Accepting scapegoating, excuses, or counterproductive behavior does not solve problems. On the contrary, it impedes the problem-solving process.

They are disrespectful toward their employees. Respect and trust are the framework of any good relationship. Any action that does not consider the feelings of employees or that is not responsive to their need to be trusted demonstrates a lack of concern for them as people. An employee who meets with this reaction will likely not feel the need to live up to a higher standard and, moreover, will likely not respect the manager who behaves in this fashion.

They fail to fulfill their promises or deny that they made promises. Breaking promises not only conveys a noncaring, insensitive attitude but also says to others that being untrustworthy is an acceptable behavior. Imagine if this were what employees learned from you, and then imagine what would happen if they were to carry these same negative behaviors over to their interactions with your customers. If employees repeatedly promise customers that they will receive a product by a certain date and then fail to follow through on these promises, you would find your customer base quickly decreasing. Instead, by setting a higher example for members of your department, you encourage similar behavior on their part and garner their trust.

They discourage forthrightness and honesty. If employees are afraid that their honesty and forthrightness will be penalized, they will be loath to express their views and thoughts, even if doing so can benefit the department. Managers can stifle forthrightness in a variety of ways, both subtle and blatant. Be careful what you say and how you act when an employee expresses an honest opinion, points out places where your department is less productive, or comes to you with what appears to be a genuine concern about another employee or situation. You must be sure that, in your words and actions, you continually foment a departmental culture that is open to positive dialogue and productive communication.

They breed negativism by accentuating what is wrong with the department, playing favorites, and speaking badly of employees to other members of the department. By harping on the negative aspects of a department, managers drive employees to play the "blame game" rather than finding ways to fix the problems so the department is more productive. By playing favorites, they exclude all nonfavorite members of the group and stir negative feelings throughout. Employees who are not receiving encouragement and supervision will not live up to their highest potential and will end up resenting the manager's "pets," while those receiving all of the manager's attention may feel entitled to benefits they did not earn and may perceive themselves as above working with and listening to their fellow employees. In the same vein, speaking badly of employees not only sets a bad example but also creates divisiveness among the staff.

You can probably think of other ways a manager can create a defensive culture. Do you find yourself exhibiting any of these behaviors? If so, give some thought to what you can do to change these negative behaviors.

Common Trappings

All of these defensive actions have certain traits in common. First, not one of these behaviors will consistently help managers or their employees solve problems. Second, they deter employees from being as productive as they can be. Remember that actions or reactions that do not lead managers or their employees one step closer to a reasonable want—a want that serves the best interests of the department—are defensive behaviors. Finally, defensive behaviors block people, and thus an entire department, from steadily moving forward. Such behaviors may have short-term value and achieve short-term results, but in the journey to success, habitual defensiveness is a dead end.

Discovery Lesson

If you are going to lead by example, you must do all you can to minimize your own defensiveness. This Discovery Lesson will help you do that. It is based on the notion that awareness is the beginning of change.

Listen carefully to people talking to each other, either at meetings or in casual conversations. Every time you hear what you deem an important conversation that is sprinkled with defensive statements, record the conversation in writing as soon as you can. Describe the scene, the people present, and the subject of the conversation, as well as actual statements. Do this for a few days. Then, transfer your notes to your manager's journal, and label the section "Defensive Statements I Overheard and What They Really Mean."

For each negative statement you noted, ask yourself these questions: Will this statement move the speaker one step closer to achieving a reasonable want? What is the point of the defensive statement? What does the speaker hope to accomplish? Will the speaker succeed in getting whatever it is he or she wants, which is *really* important to this person?

In most cases, you'll recognize that the negative statements you overheard are a waste of time, energy, and emotion. This is because defensiveness of any sort may satisfy one's emotions, but it doesn't resolve the problem that triggered the defensiveness. The only thing that was accomplished was that the employee blew off some steam.

Characteristics of a Problem-Solving Culture

In a problem-solving culture, managers assume that their employees are responsible, and they treat them accordingly. Furthermore, employees know, either instinctively or because they've been taught, that their main function is to solve problems and produce results. To do so, they should be primed by the manager to ask themselves the following questions whenever they face a problem:

- What specifically do I want? Is it reasonable (i.e., attainable)?
- Do I have a detailed plan for achieving my reasonable wants? If I anticipate barriers that could interfere with reaching my objectives, does my plan describe how I could overcome those barriers?
- Am I committed to working through my plan methodically and conscientiously?
- How will I determine whether or not I'm on track? How frequently should I follow up?

- If negative thoughts or outside influences are sidetracking me, what specifically can I do to rid myself of those thoughts and influences?

In a problem-solving culture, these questions enable employees to progress from point A, which is where they are, to point B, which is where they want to go. (A facsimile of this problem-solving process is included in the Appendix.)

A variation of this problem-solving model, in which you help the employee through the process, is also effective under certain conditions. Suppose, for example, Harry comes to you and says, "I've got a problem and I need your help." You can provide assistance through one of two methods, either by helping analyze symptoms or by helping assess options.

Method 1: Analyze the Symptoms

If the employee is upset about an incident but does not seem to have a clear understanding of the root of the problem or is having trouble articulating it, you would use this method. Ask him to describe the symptoms of the problem. Ask what he thinks might be causing the symptoms. Ask what he might do to solve the problem. Discuss alternative solutions with him, if necessary.

Method 2: Assess the Options

If the employee seems to have a handle on the cause of the problem but isn't able to see a solution, you would use this method. You might ask him to mentally work through his options and then discuss each one. An alternative is for you to bring some options to his attention and then discuss with him the pros and cons of each.

Each method reflects the basic philosophy of a problem-solving culture, which is that all employees are worthy of respect. A good manager respects employees' emotions, options, and abilities to solve problems on their own or with some coaching.

When a well-regarded company president was asked to explain the secret of his success, he said, "I strip people of any excuses they might have for not performing well by giving them everything they need from me to perform to the best of their abilities. I don't want to be anyone's excuse for not fulfilling responsibilities. Without excuses, those who don't have the desire to succeed will leave."

We have heard variations of this philosophy during our years of consulting with companies whose managers succeeded in creating problem-solving cultures. The main attitude each of them had in common is a genuine regard for the people under their influence. They want them to succeed. So, they do whatever is necessary to help them achieve that objective. Their genuine caring attitude is expressed in a variety of ways, with both words and actions, all of which say to the people in their departments that they are vital and valuable contributors to the group. These successful managers also provide employees with the tools and resources required for them to succeed.

The following are some of the specific attitudes and actions that successful managers we've known encourage in their departments and companies:

- Be willing to take risks.
- Be helpful to your fellow employees.
- Focus on how you can solve problems, not on blaming others for causing them.
- Be trustworthy.
- Be a conscientious student of your fellow employees and the people you serve, because everyone has something to teach.

Comparing Defensive and Problem-Solving Cultures

Defensive Cultures

- Characterized by fearful attitudes.

- Manager has all the answers.

- People are mainly concerned with who is right.

- People focus on personalities.

- People ask questions that place others on the defensive.

- Risk taking is discouraged.

- Problems are stated in negative terms.

- People complain about what they're not getting.

- People view themselves as victims.

- People are resistant to change.

- People are close-minded.

Problem-Solving Cultures

- Characterized by genuine caring attitudes.

- Manager asks astute questions; manager is a student of the employees.

- People are mainly concerned with what is right.

- People focus on issues and solutions.

- People ask questions that lead to solutions.

- Risk taking is encouraged.

- Problems are stated in positive terms.

- People ask: "How can I accomplish X so I can get Y?"

- People view themselves as being in control of their problems.

- People are responsive to change.

- People are open-minded.

- Avoid asking questions that place people on the defensive.
- Be sensitive toward others.

As is evident when you compare defensive cultures with problem-solving cultures (see page 76), the former stifle productivity and growth, while the latter encourage employees to be the best they can be. This comparison clearly demonstrates why successful managers are successful.

Questions to Consider

- *Am I inadvertently doing anything to create a defensive culture in my department? If I am, what can I do to change this to a problem-solving department?*

- *How can I keep my employees from falling into the trap of being defensive?*

- *How can I encourage my employees to be "problem solvers" rather than "defenders"?*

7

Discourage Enemies from Invading Your Departmental Garden

THE SINGLE TOUGHEST CHALLENGE of gardeners is to make sure weeds, as well as harmful insects, don't make the garden their permanent home. The reasons are obvious if you've ever seen a weed- and bug-infested garden. Not only do weeds rob gardens of vital nutrients, but harmful worms and bugs also feast on beautiful plants and hearty vegetables as if they were theirs. These intruders, if allowed to take control, will prevent the garden from thriving.

For the sake of simplicity, this chapter refers to all types of garden enemies as weeds. Weeds detract from a garden's beauty, and they require time and energy to eradicate—time and energy that could be used to promote the growth of your desired plants. In applying the analogy to your departmental culture, keep in mind this dictionary definition:

A weed is a valueless, troublesome, or noxious plant growing wild, especially one that grows profusely or on cultivated ground to the exclusion or injury of the desired crop.

Don't Let Weeds Take Root

Just as gardens have weeds, so do organizations. Much the same way weeds in your garden will affect the growth of your plants and not allow them to flourish, organizational weeds will adversely affect profits, morale, and productivity in your department. As a manager within your organization, you have the power to prevent weeds from infiltrating your turf. That's a power you must exercise if you are to fulfill your mission, which is to create a profitable, productive department staffed by people with positive attitudes.

Of course, weeds, by their very nature, crop up uninvited and without warning. But you can prevent them from taking root and proliferating by creating a departmental atmosphere that is open and honest and takes a problem-solving approach to disagreements and differences of opinion.

Preventing weeds from appearing and taking root in your departmental garden will be well worth your time and effort. In a culture that's reasonably weed-free, ideas flourish, productivity is high, cooperation is second nature, quality performance is a source of pride, and team spirit continuously motivates employees to excel. These enticing benefits should spur you to create such a culture. However, in order to do so, you have to recognize weeds when you see them, prevent them from spreading, and discourage new ones from growing.

Identifying Departmental Weeds

In Chapter 1, you wrote a mission statement that included guidelines for creating the departmental culture that you and your employees envisioned. Anything that disrupts or inhibits this mission is a weed. To ensure that your mission and vision are truly effective, you must discourage weeds from invading your departmental garden. The first order of business is learning to recognize the four general qualities and characteristics of a departmental weed: A weed is any action or reaction that does not contribute to the betterment of your department, that does not reflect your mission statement, that undermines your problem-solving philosophy, or that hurts the department as a whole or any individual in the department.

Departmental weeds, being tricky little devils, take a variety of forms; some are easy to identify, and some lurk below the surface. This section describes a handful of the more common examples. These may be characteristics that you exhibit as manager or that you note in your employees. In either case, it will be advantageous to you to be able to recognize them in order to dislodge them from your department. As you read each description, ask yourself if you can cite specific examples of this negative behavior in your own department.

Defensiveness. Defensiveness of any sort is potentially the single most pernicious weed. Examples of defensive behavior are blaming, finding fault, and making excuses; such actions sabotage the problem-solving process. When people are defensive, they act irresponsibly and emotionally. As a consequence, activities may be stalled or not completed to your level of satisfaction. Defensiveness hinders productivity.

Labeling. An employee comes to you with the complaint that a coworker is ineffective, or irresponsible, or sloppy, or rude. These negative labels don't say anything meaningful about the person or situation in question. Instead of indicating how the coworker is being ineffective and what steps need to be taken to remedy the situation, the employee is simply expressing anger and frustration. Negative labeling is not a productive behavior.

Negativism. Negativism breeds negativism and demoralizes the culture where it's allowed. Whether you say to an employee, or one employee says to another, "This won't work" or "That's a bad idea," or an individual feels as if nothing he or she does will make a difference, negativism has the power to cloud employees' positive outlooks and dissuade them from risk taking and excelling.

Close-Mindedness. If employees sense that you've made up your mind about something without giving them the chance to present their opinions, or if, in general, you tend to make decisions without asking for others' thoughts, you will be viewed as close-minded. This is also a sign that you do not value your employees and do not respect their contributions to your department. Similarly, no one employee should be so certain that his or her way is the right way that the person is not willing to discuss others' ideas. Close-minded responses to any logical argument are certain to impede positive communication between you and the members of the department.

Impatience. Impatience can be expressed in many ways. You or your employees may expect more from someone than the person is capable of giving and become frustrated and impatient with the person. Or you may expect too much too soon and give up on the struggling employee prematurely. As is the case with some plants, certain people require more time to develop or grow and thus require more of your patience in order to fulfill their potential. People also have varying abilities and aptitudes; it is unfair and unreasonable to assume that everyone has the same potential, can excel in the same manner, and works at the same pace.

Refusing Responsibility. You will fail your department if you refuse to take responsibility for wrongs. Likewise, your employees should not be averse to accepting responsibility for their actions. Before a problem can be solved, someone has to shoulder responsibility for it and then ensure that a course of action will be taken to rectify the situation. Passing the buck will not accomplish anything and will lead to an infinite circle of blame.

Distrust. Employees will sense your distrust of them and their abilities if you micromanage, if you do not delegate work when appropriate, if you do not ask for opinions when appropriate, or if they feel that you are not giving them the freedom to do their jobs as they see fit. Again, distrust inhibits risk taking and initiative in your employees.

Untrustworthiness. This is typically one of the easiest weeds to identify. If an employee is not fulfilling his or her responsibilities, not honoring promises, failing to maintain confidences, or initiating or spreading rumors, then this individual is creating an atmosphere in which nothing can be taken at face value. The cohesiveness of your department will be undermined if this network of untrustworthiness is allowed to proliferate.

All behaviors, either yours or your employees', that do not contribute to the growth of your department as a whole are harmful to your objectives. It is your job to recognize these problematic behaviors and attitudes and remove them from the workplace. If you can accomplish this, your mission statement will become a reality.

Now that you know how to identify them, you're ready to learn how to keep weeds from taking root in your department. This is the topic of the next section.

Discovery Lesson

Be aware of any weedlike behaviors that are particular to your department, and note them in your manager's journal. Review the eight negative traits detailed in the preceding section, and try to match each to the actions of an employee or other associate from your current or former workplace. The purpose of this activity is not to dwell on negative behaviors but to be able to identify them. The more adept you are at recognizing them, the better you will become at resolving them using the tools discussed in this book.

Discouraging Enemies from Harming Your Department

When you accepted the responsibility of departmental manager, you made certain implied promises that you must now fulfill. The most important implied promise was to create a culture in which each employee has an opportunity to realize his or her potential.

That opportunity grows out of meaningful challenges, a cooperative and positive atmosphere, encouragement and appropriate direction from you, and freedom from negative forces—or weeds—that can interfere with employees' effectiveness.

Creating a totally weed-free departmental culture is idealistic and, therefore, impossible. People are imperfect and often are influenced by their nonrational emotions. Nevertheless, you can strive to create a culture similar to the one that your own "best manager" developed.

The process begins with a statement to the department expressing your desire and asking for each employee's help to achieve it. Using your own words, the message you want to get across is essentially this:

"In addition to the departmental mission, which is expressed in our mission statement, I, as manager of the department, have my own private mission. It is to create an environment in which all employees feel motivated to perform their respective jobs to the best of their abilities and are encouraged to act responsibly toward one another. To ensure that both of these objectives are fulfilled, distractions, which are like weeds in a garden, must be reduced to a minimum."

Clarify for your employees that a "weed" is any action or reaction that does not serve the best interests of the department and its employees. You can refer to the four characteristics of a weed presented earlier in the chapter, and you may even want to distribute copies of the description so that employees can have it readily available as a reminder. (See the Appendix for reproducible text.)

The final step in reducing the opportunities for weeds to enter your departmental garden is requesting that employees take responsibility for being problem solvers and avoiding negative, weedlike behaviors. If every person in the department, including you, makes a conscious effort to create a positive, fertile working environment that's free of weeds, then everyone will benefit.

In addition to expressing this message to your current employees, when you hire new people, make sure they are problem solvers and not prone to defensiveness. Although you can never be 100 percent sure of hiring people who are free of weedlike inclinations, you can increase your chances by listening carefully to their responses to your questions. In particular, listen to their descriptions of how they handle adversity. Telltale signs include shifting blame, finding fault, making excuses, and failing to take responsibility for mistakes.

During your interviews with prospective employees, you may also want to tell them that your private mission is to create an environment in which all employees feel motivated to perform to the best of their abilities and are encouraged to act responsibly toward one another. Then ask candidates how they can contribute to the fulfillment of this mission. If you get a favorable response, you're probably looking at someone who would be a healthy addition to that environment.

How to Deal with Stubborn Weeds

Creating an open and productive working environment is an ambitious undertaking. While conscientious employees will embrace this fresh outlook, others will stubbornly resist it. They may be mired in their old habits of blaming and finding fault with others, bullying fellow employees, and allowing their egos to dictate their actions. Since these actions are harmful to your department, it is imperative that you put a stop to them.

To help you discourage people who insist on generating weeds, you might want to enlist the aid of other members of your department. Perhaps a "Weed-Control Committee" can be formed to protect the culture you worked so hard to create from deteriorating. The more people you involve in a cause that is beneficial to everyone in your department, the more successful it will be. You may find that the merits extend beyond your department to the whole organization. Wouldn't that be a kick?

If all your positive efforts fail with someone you're certain is a weed producer, and you've put the person on notice, you have only one resort: uproot the weed. It is better to remove a weed than to allow it to ruin your garden.

Tips and techniques for delivering bad news and managing uncomfortable situations are provided in subsequent chapters.

Questions to Consider

- *What are some examples of weedlike behaviors in my department?*

- *Who in my department could help me form a weed-control committee or will actively promote my positive ideals?*

- *How else can I deflect enemies from invading my departmental garden?*

PART II

Building on Your Foundation

Creating a solid departmental foundation is a good start toward fulfilling your responsibilities as a professional manager. But it is only a start. Now that you have learned how to lay the groundwork for a positive, productive department that consists of energetic employees who are eager to take risks and work together, you need to learn how to successfully build on your solid foundation.

In this part of the book, you will learn how to constructively criticize employees so that they view the criticism as a gift. All too often, criticisms are confused with adverse judgments. The objective of the former is to be helpful and to improve upon a situation, while the objective of the latter is only to highlight shortcomings.

For criticisms to be received as gifts, they have to be properly packaged and presented.

You will also gain insight into the art of asking questions. There are right and wrong ways to ask questions. Right ways will help you and your employees achieve your objectives, while wrong ways will cause your employees to be defensive. You will learn how to ask questions that allow you to connect with your employees and help them solve problems.

You will learn how to hire people who will add value to your department. Your department's effectiveness depends on the quality of the people who compose it. With sound preparation and practice, you can recruit personnel who are ready, willing, and able to perform the functions of the job.

You will learn how to conduct performance reviews that benefit your employees. Performance reviews, when done right, help employees improve their skills and develop qualities that will make them more effective.

You will learn how to conduct productive departmental meetings. Departmental meetings can easily become a waste of time. Or they can be useful and productive gatherings. Everyone involved will benefit from these meetings once you know what specifically you need to do to make them more productive.

You will find out how to make it safe for your staff to take reasonable risks. As a manager, you must encourage your employees to expand their comfort zones. If you don't, you stymie their contributions to your department. You must also teach them how to assess which risks are reasonable and which ones should not be taken.

You will discover how to delegate effectively. Because you can't do everything yourself, knowing how to share work with employees is essential. But, as with everything else you do as a manager, you must delegate correctly, in the proper terms and with the proper attitude, and to the right people. You need to know how to identify which employees can handle certain tasks and which ones cannot.

You'll develop mastery in resolving conflicts. Differences in perceptions and opinions often create conflicts. No matter how solid your departmental foundation, conflicts will seep through. That's to be expected, and as long as they are resolved and lead to win-win outcomes, they do not signify a weakness within your department.

You will learn how to deal with and prevent harassment. Sexual harassment is not the only type that plagues companies. Regardless of the nature of the harassment you encounter, you must know how to prevent it from harming your work environment and your employees.

By applying the knowledge you will gain in these chapters, which complements what you learned in Part 1, you will accomplish two important objectives: you will create a model department, one in which employees are productive and are encouraged to grow, and by helping them grow, you will prepare them for future supervisory or managerial positions.

Let's move forward.

A soft answer turns away wrath, but a harsh word stirs anger.

Criticism is a valuable gift. But, to be viewed as such, it must be properly wrapped and sensitively presented.

It is kinder to be gently direct than to be cruelly silent.

8

Give the Gift of Constructive Criticism

WHAT WOULD YOU DO IF an employee exercised poor judgment in handling a problem? What would you do if an employee failed to meet your expectations? What would you do if you were disappointed with an employee who did not fulfill a promise?

The hard truth is that when an employee does something that is harmful to your department's culture, or does something you know is wrong, you must let the person know. In such cases, you have the specific obligation to tell your employees what they did wrong, explain why the action disappointed you, provide whatever help they need to correct the situation, and make sure they understand what they can do to prevent a recurrence.

But how do you correct an employee without being offensive? How do you criticize without being critical? How do you confront without being confrontational? The answers to those questions are the subject of this chapter.

Change Begins with Awareness

Put yourself in the employee's shoes for a moment: Imagine you are an employee who inadvertently has not fulfilled several of your manager's expectations, or who exercised poor judgment in handling a customer complaint, or who did something else that is unacceptable to your manager. How would you want your manager to address the situation? Here are four possible responses:

- Ignore your actions so as not to hurt your feelings.
- Chastise you, either privately or in front of your colleagues, and make you feel guilty or stupid.
- Tell you what you did wrong but offer no suggestions for improving.
- Call your attention to what you did or didn't do that was unacceptable, determine the cause of your misdemeanor, agree on a course of corrective action, and discuss what needs to be done to prevent the problem from recurring.

Clearly, the last reaction is what you would expect of a professional manager. This tactic is both effective and benevolent. It is effective in that the manager confronts you with your errors rather than allowing you to believe that everything is fine. It is benevolent because it involves you in the solution to a problem of your own making. That is a thoughtful gift, don't you agree?

This is what your employees have a right to expect from you. They trust you to tell them how they can improve their performance. They also trust you not to collect bricks or to build invisible walls. In short, they trust you to be forthright and supportive, and to do everything in your power to help them succeed.

If you do not fairly criticize or confront employees when it's appropriate, you are setting them up to fail. How can people improve if they're unaware that they did something wrong? Awareness is the beginning of change. As their manager, you must make your employees aware of their shortcomings and mistakes, and provide them with the guidance they need to improve and correct their errors. You must not deprive them of gifts that can make them better employees and people.

Although helpful criticism is a valuable gift, many managers lack the courage to offer it. That's because they confuse criticism with adverse judgments and, therefore, equate it to a personal assault. They assume that the recipient would feel hurt and become defensive. It follows that criticism given by managers who harbor such negative views invariably triggers the very reaction they fear: defensiveness and anger.

However, it's not criticism itself that engenders such reactions. They occur because of the way the criticism is offered. The reactions these reluctant managers receive from their criticism are examples of a negative self-fulfilling prophecy.

Suppose these same managers came to view criticism as gifts they give to people for whom they have a genuine regard, or as an aid in their employees' development, or as a vital part of their responsibility to help their employees be the best they can be. Suppose they assumed their employees would be grateful. You can be certain that those views and assumptions would also prove to be a self-fulfilling prophecy. But, being a positive prophecy, the "gifts" would be properly wrapped, sensitively presented, and, therefore, gratefully received.

As a professional manager, you must convince yourself that warranted criticism can benefit your employees. You must believe that your employees trust you to give them gifts of criticism. They trust you because deep within, they know your intentions are honorable. You must also assume that when you fail to criticize employees when it is warranted, you are inadvertently sabotaging them. Finally, you must be less concerned with your feelings about criticizing than in doing the right thing in the right way for the sake of your employees.

Here's a real-life testimony, from a child's perspective: A ten-year-old boy was describing his relationship with his parents and siblings. When he got around to talking about his father, he said, "My dad doesn't love me." When asked why he said that, he answered, "Because he never yells at me, even when I do wrong."

We're not suggesting that you yell at employees when they do wrong, just to show them you care. What we do recommend is that you care enough about them to call their attention to unacceptable work performance and actions rather than ignore those behaviors. Be a gift giver.

How to Present Your Gifts Properly

Remember that we are talking about criticism, not adverse judgments. Whereas adverse judgments only make a person feel bad, guilty, or stupid, criticism aims to be helpful and to solve problems.

To reiterate, criticism should accomplish three objectives:

- Make the person you're criticizing aware of what you see and why it's a problem for you.
- Show the person you're criticizing what changes will alleviate the problem.
- Increase the likelihood that the behavior won't recur.

To achieve those objectives, you need the cooperation of the other party. You will likely gain employees' cooperation if you treat them as friends and if you obey certain guidelines.

First, make sure your criticism identifies the specific problem that concerns you. For example, suppose an employee submits a report to you that's riddled with spelling errors. Your criticism might be, "It bothers me to receive a report that's filled with spelling mistakes." Or suppose an employee is demanding of the department secretary. You might say, "I believe in treating every member of the department with respect. That's why it bothers me when you make demands of our secretary."

Second, make sure you tell the employee what specifically you want that would resolve your problem. Concerning the error-filled report, you could say, "Your reports would look more professional if you used the spell check that's available to you" or "Before handing in a report to me, make sure there are no spelling errors." In the example of the demanding employee, you could say, "When making a request of our secretary, ask for what you need, rather than tell her, in a demanding voice, what you want. As my grandmother used to say, You can catch more flies with honey than with vinegar."

Third, make sure you agree on how to prevent the problem from recurring. (This guideline is flexible and may not always be applicable.) For example, "Could we agree that you will proofread your reports before you give them to me?" or "Could we agree that any expenditure above X dollars should be checked with me?"

To help you incorporate constructive criticism as a teaching tool, adopt the following attitudes:

- Criticisms are gifts that I don't want to withhold from people about whom I genuinely care. It's my responsibility as a manager to provide them with my gifts of criticism.
- My duty is to tell the person I'm criticizing what specifically I want, need, or expect, without adversely judging anyone as a prelude to the request.
- Never criticize emotions, since emotions are neither right nor wrong.
- Only criticize behavior, never the person.
- It is kinder to be gently direct than cruelly silent.

Discovery Lesson

In your manager's journal, describe three expectations that were unfulfilled by people who work for you.

Now pretend you want to confront each of these employees regarding the respective behavior. For each unfulfilled expectation, take two approaches: (1) Be a friend, and criticize constructively; present the person you're criticizing with a well-packaged, attractively wrapped, and useful gift. (2) Adversely judge the action, not the person.

Remember: Criticisms are helpful gifts. Let's say, for example, an employee promised to submit a report. The due date arrives, and no report is forthcoming. When you go to your employee to request it, she says she hasn't got it but she'll get it to you in a few days. You must inform her that this behavior is unacceptable. At the same time, you want her to know what is acceptable behavior.

This is what the criticism might sound like: "When you tell me you'll do something, I expect you to do it. I want to trust you, but you have to prove yourself trustworthy by fulfilling your promises. Next time, if you see that you can't deliver what you promised, tell me in advance so I can work around the change. Is that a reasonable request?"

Adverse judgments are statements that chastise and, either intentionally or unintentionally, make the person being judged feel bad and prompt defensiveness. Typically, adverse judgments begin with "You" and are followed by negative comments.

Using the same example, this is what an adverse judgment would sound like: "You didn't fulfill your promise to me. How could you be so irresponsible? You really let me down by not doing what you were supposed to when you were supposed to do it."

After completing this Discovery Lesson, reflect on what you learned and record your insights in your journal.

How to Gain Cooperation from Other Managers Without Being Critical

There will be times when you need the cooperation of other managers but are not getting it. Usually, these noncooperative managers will tell you they are too busy and can't spare the time. Although you may be angry and be tempted to criticize (actually, adversely judge) them, or to give them a piece of your mind, that's not a good idea. Doing so would likely spoil your chances of getting what you want or need from them. Would you be cooperative if another manager placed you on the defensive? Probably not.

In such cases, criticism is inappropriate. Managers would consider it insulting to be told by another manager what they should or shouldn't do, or what is proper and improper behavior when dealing with a fellow manager. Even if your advice is sound, there is slim hope that they will take it as a gift.

So, resist the temptation of criticizing noncooperative fellow managers. Keep your eyes on your objective, which is to obtain what you need from them. Make it easy for them to give you what you want. Don't hand them an excuse to reject you.

An approach that has been successful is based on the premise that your anger at not getting what you need from a fellow manager does not have to be expressed as a criticism. This is how it works:

Ask the manager whose help you need to give you a few minutes to discuss an issue. Most people won't deny you that. Then, when you meet, say something to this effect:

"Like you, my staff and I want to do the best job we know how. To achieve that objective, we need your help. I know your department is busy, just as we are, but without your cooperation, we're going to fall short of what we need to accomplish. What can I say or do to gain your department's cooperation?"

By all means, use your own words. However you phrase it, make your request positive. Never make your counterpart feel that he or she hasn't been cooperative.

In summary, your ultimate objective as manager is to increase your department's value by doing all you can to improve the quality and effectiveness of the people under your influence. Criticizing, not adversely judging, them when it's appropriate is the kindest, most generous way of saying, "Since you matter to me, I want you to be the best you can be. My criticisms are gifts that will help you achieve that objective."

Questions to Consider

- *How do you plan to remind yourself that adverse judgments are hurtful, while criticisms are helpful?*

- *Why would it not be appropriate to criticize an uncooperative fellow manager?*

- *It's easy to confuse helpful criticism with lecturing to a person whose behavior needs correction. What's the difference between the two?*

> *Don't allow past pains and disappointments to hold your future hostage.*
>
> *When your emotions take control, your brain becomes disengaged.*

9

Resolving Conflicts

THE PREVIOUS EIGHT CHAPTERS INTRODUCED THE principles, tools, and skills for building strong interpersonal relationships and creating a healthy departmental environment. This environment is referred to as a problem-solving culture, as opposed to a defensive culture.

Assuming you have consistently applied those principles, tools, and skills, you discovered how to make conscientious employees thrive and how to stimulate the department to flourish. That's because, in addition to encouraging your employees to be the best they can be, you encourage them to cooperate with each other to achieve their individual and common objectives. By applying what you learned, you harnessed the power of the knowledge and skills you gained.

You learned how to be respectful and trustworthy, how to listen effectively, how to criticize without being critical, how to solve problems, how to develop and perpetuate positive attitudes, how to discourage defensiveness, how to ask the right questions in the right way, and more. All of these skills are also useful in dealing with and resolving conflicts. To complement this inventory, you will need a few additional skills to effectively manage conflicts. Helping you develop those skills is the subject of this chapter.

A legitimate question here is, If I've succeeded in creating a healthy environment, why would I still encounter conflicts in my department? The answer is that conflicts are normal occurrences in any group where people work together, live together, are dependent on one another to achieve their individual and common objectives, vie for attention, or compete for the same rewards.

Thus, conflicts will occur between your employees as well as between you and them. Helping conflicting parties resolve their differences to their mutual satisfaction is essential to your success.

The Nature of Conflicts

Conflicts are products of our uniqueness. Being unique, each of us views the same environment and the same experiences differently. We also confront problems differently and have different opinions, values, and needs. Those differences in and of themselves do not necessarily cause conflicts. What causes conflicts is how we respond to and act out our differences. Attitudes such as "You're wrong and I'm right," "You're my enemy, whom I must conquer," and "I'm in charge, so we'll do it my way," as well as any other defensive or combative attitudes, make resolution difficult, if not impossible.

In contrast, you will increase the likelihood of helping parties resolve a conflict if, before they begin the resolution process, you direct them to adopt the following attitudes:

- A conflict is a problem. Like all problems, this one needs to be resolved so that we can move forward.
- I genuinely want to resolve our conflict.
- A conflict is only one element of a relationship. We're not in conflict with each other; we're in conflict with only some aspect of our relationship.
- I am willing to continue discussing our issues until both of us are satisfied with the solution to which we agree. That is, we both must get what we want, what we deem reasonable, before we end our discussion.
- I want us both to benefit from our solution.
- Since I don't want us to be combative, I promise to work together with you rather than defend my ego.

These attitudes, which reflect a positive view of conflicts, suggest that conflicts are opportunities for the people involved to learn about each other's needs, desires, perceptions, and goals. They also are opportunities to explore how seemingly conflicting parties can work together to zero in on their respective goals.

As evidence of the potential positive nature of conflicts, consider the conflicts we frequently have with ourselves. For example, let's say you are a successful salesperson and you enjoy your job. Because of your success, you are offered a position as sales manager. You face what is called an approach-approach conflict. That is, you want to continue to sell, but you also want the promotion. Confronting this choice, you have to thoroughly examine what's best for you and why.

A second example depicts what is called an approach-avoidance conflict. Here, you've been offered a high-paying job as a consultant for a company that sells computer software. The work is appealing to you, as is the money, but the job entails 50 percent out-of-town travel. That does not appeal to you, since you have a family consisting of a spouse and three children, and you don't want to be away from them for long stretches.

Finally, you may have an avoidance-avoidance conflict, which is characterized by the adage "caught between the devil and the deep blue sea." For instance, you are offered a promotion that requires you to relocate, something you don't want to do for personal reasons. However, if you don't accept the promotion, you will have to remain in your current job, which you no longer find challenging.

In all three conflicts, as you weigh your choices you learn about yourself. You learn what's important and unimportant to you, what you like and dislike, what you need to be happy with your life, what your values are and their relative strengths, and more.

Similarly, interpersonal conflicts can also be useful if you and your employees approach them as opportunities to learn and grow.

Three Examples of Conflicts

Review the following common workplace situations, and at the end of the chapter, determine your corresponding responses under "Questions to Consider."

Example 1: Performance Rating

A month ago, you assigned one of your employees, Josh, a project, which he enthusiastically accepted. After completing it, he submitted a written report of what he did and the results he came up with. Now you are going to with him to discuss the report and your evaluation of his performance.

Josh believes he did an excellent job. You, however, rate the work he did, as well as his report, as only fair. You and Josh have a conflict in perception. (Before answering the corresponding question at the end of this chapter, you may want to review Chapter 8 on constructive criticism.)

Example 2: Group Consensus

A committee consisting of four professors and a chairperson develops a teacher evaluation form for the school's management department. The final document they will propose is acceptable to all five committee members. When they present the form at the next faculty meeting, ten faculty members approve it, but four do not. These are the reactions of the four dissenters:

Chuck: I don't like it.
Marvin: I don't like it either.
Millie: It's too short.
Jane: It's not specific enough.

You are among the group of ten who approved. You are now expected to help resolve the individual conflicts with Chuck, Marvin, Millie, and Jane and then gain consensus from the entire faculty present at the meeting.

Example 3: Meeting Expectations

Fred, the sales manager of a medium-size computer software company, has three salespeople working for him. About six months ago, the three employees requested a meeting with Fred to discuss their mutual expectations. At the end of the two-hour meeting, they all agreed on mutual expectations that they determined to be reasonable. All parties felt that they had a good understanding of what the salespeople wanted from the manager and what the manager wanted from the salespeople.

Within three months of that meeting, the salespeople became frustrated by the manager's failure to honor one of their key agreements, which was to be available to discuss sensitive customer-related issues. That failure marred the salespeople's efforts. In some instances, the manager's lack of availability proved costly.

Angered by the situation, the salespeople now schedule a confrontation with the manager. You are one of the salespeople and must present your case to your manager.

Other Types of Conflicts

Conflicts come in all shapes and in various degrees of complexity. What follows are general descriptions of some familiar types. For each, think of actual examples from your own experience; write them down in your journal under the appropriate headings, as described earlier in this chapter.

- Two people have the same objective but can't seem to agree on a procedure for achieving it. What they want to accomplish is the same; how they want to accomplish it is different.
- Two people consider their respective views or positions on a critical issue threatening to each other. Each believes that relenting will undermine his or her image.
- Two people's goals are not only different but also mutually exclusive. If we do A, we can't do B, and vice versa.

- Two people have different beliefs of what is right and proper concerning a sensitive employee matter.
- Two people who don't like each other have to work together on a project. Their only possible course of action is to find a way of completing the project to the best of their abilities.
- Your evaluation of what one of your employees contributes to the department is different from the employee's own evaluation.
- A person tries to impose his or her opinion or values on another person.
- Conflicting parties differ in the way they treat people.
- The needs of two people working together are not being met to the satisfaction of either.

Strategies for Dealing with Conflicts

Whether you are mediating a conflict between coworkers or are directly involved in a conflict with an employee or with a manager from another department, the following approaches can serve you well when applied judiciously.

- Ask appropriate questions. Let's use the reaction of Marvin at the faculty meeting in the preceding group consensus example. Marvin says, "I don' like it either." The following questions would help resolve the conflict:

     When you say "it," Marvin, what specifically are you referring to?

     What changes would make it more acceptable to you?

     Are there any other specific concerns you have?

     If we make those changes, would the evaluation form be acceptable to you?

Questions such as these are intended to nail down the nature of the conflict. They are appropriate whenever a party to a conflict uses generalizations or abstractions. Here, "it" could easily be misinterpreted as meaning the whole form when in fact only one element—say, the introductory paragraph or the typeface— is objectionable.

- Confront the conflicting party. Confrontations should not be viewed as anything more than positive attempts to settle problems. They are necessary means for resolving differences. Let's say April expects June to fulfill a promise that June made to provide a mailing list. Several days go by and the list is not forwarded.

   It would be appropriate for April to confront June with a statement such as, "I've got a problem. I believe you promised to give me a mailing list yesterday. I'm sure it was an oversight, but when do you think I can have it? It's important that I get it as soon as possible."

   As you can see, this is a confrontation, but there is nothing combative about the overture.

- Pose your dissonance. Frequently, conflicts arise when a person's actions are not in harmony with his or her words. If you experienced such disharmony with a vendor, for example, you could pose your dissonance to your representative by saying, "I'm confused. You said that you value me as a customer, but when I come to you with a problem, I am not given the respect I believe I deserve. Would you please unconfuse me?" In this way, you force that person to take responsibility for resolving your problem.

   Another tack might be, "If what you're saying is true, how do you explain the fact that my last two phone calls were not returned?"

- Present evidence to support your position, then ask for evidence that supports the other party's position. Assuming a conflicting party doesn't take the unreasonable stance of "I have got my mind made up, regardless of any facts that may cause me to think again," facts can be useful in bringing antagonists closer to concurrence.

- Be flexible. In the interest of ensuring that conflicting parties achieve their mutual objectives, both will have to give a little— but not grudgingly. Giving is not the same as giving up. When you give, it's a voluntary gesture of goodwill, whereas giving up is an admission of weakness or failure. Giving up is usually done with resentment, while giving reflects a caring attitude.

- Define the components of a conflict. A frequently voiced complaint between conflicting parties is, "I can't work with that person because we have a personality conflict." This comment is meaningless until the specific objection is made clear. What does it mean when two people have a "personality conflict"? What are the components of that conflict? Only by defining the conflict in terms of what the parties need that they're not getting from each other can they settle it.

- Focus on mutual objectives, not on personalities. To move in a productive direction, answer this question: If the relationship between the conflicting parties were perfect, what specific needs would be fulfilled? Focus on those needs.

- Establish how each party would benefit from a resolution.

- Take small, nonthreatening steps, agreeable to both parties, that will lead to a desirable outcome.

- If possible, compose a written agreement concerning the resolution. Having a written agreement often prompts people to take their promises more seriously than they would otherwise.

The ideal goal of a conflict resolution is to achieve agreements that benefit both parties and strengthen the relationship of the conflicting parties. You will contribute to the well-being of your department if you teach your employees how to work through their conflicts with one another.

Questions to Consider

- *How would you resolve the conflict in perception between you and Josh in Example 1 in this chapter?*

- *How would you resolve the conflicts with Chuck, Marvin, Millie, and Jane individually and as a group in Example 2? How would you gain consensus from the entire department?*

- *What is your initial statement to the sales manager in Example 3? How would you end your meeting?*

- *Describe a recent conflict that you experienced. If you resolved it successfully, how did you do it? If you didn't, what did you do that you shouldn't have? If you had to do it over, what would you do differently?*

10

How to Handle Harassment

HARASSMENT IS JUST PLAIN WRONG; there is never a valid reason or a good excuse for it. There is no way to justify harassment in any situation at any time with any person. During the course of your career as a manager, odds are you'll come into contact with a situation that qualifies as harassment. It seems that businesses face an ever-increasing number of harassment lawsuits every day. While this book does not address specific legalities or policies and procedures that are typically unique to each company, this chapter offers guiding principles for recognizing and dealing with harassment in its many forms.

Defining Harassment

A chief difficulty in dealing with harassment is simply developing an all-encompassing definition of the act. The predicament is similar to the ongoing debate among lawmakers regarding pornography. One of the more memorable quotes to come out of those debates is, "I can't define it, but I know it when I see it." Harassment, likewise, is an elusive presence that keeps the courts full and human resources departments busy. Dictionary definitions of the term include phrases such as "to trouble by repeated attacks"; "to continually disturb"; and "to torment, pester, badger, or vex." These definitions suggest that harassers victimize their targets by repeatedly violating their privacy and invading their space. Even when they're asked or told not to do whatever they're doing, harassers disregard such requests.

Everyone is entitled to privacy and space without having to justify it or earn it. As a manager, you must assure everyone in your department that you will not tolerate harassment. To back up this assurance, you must handle the problem if it arises. You do this by first being aware of it and then acting appropriately. Let's begin by looking at two examples.

Example 1: Off-Color Jokes

One of your employees, Jana, has made it clear to fellow staff members that she is offended by off-color jokes. Joel, another person in your department, gets a kick out of telling such jokes. He seems to gain particular pleasure from seeking out Jana to recite his newest gag. Although she has pleaded with him to stop, he continues to ignore her request. In fact, the more offended she becomes, the more he does it.

Example 2: Unwelcome Contact

Melvin and Harriet are coworkers in your department. Although Harriet persists in joining Melvin at the lunch table every day, Mel has made it a point to ignore her and to seek other company. This has been going on for about two weeks. Recently, Harriet called Melvin at home several times just "to make small talk." Melvin has told her that he doesn't appreciate those calls and even finds them disturbing. He also told her that he would appreciate it if she would find other people to sit with at lunch. All of these requests have fallen on deaf ears. Harriet even told him that he's being "overly sensitive" and mean.

Actions such as those of Joel and Harriet would qualify as harassment. Both examples reflect the harassers' major motivation, which is to gratify themselves at the expense of others.

A simplified way to look at harassment is as selfish behavior by a person who places more value on his or her desires and interests than on another's right to privacy. Such people consider their own feelings to be more important than those of someone else. Harassment can relate to sex, race, age, religion, size, physical ability, hair color, nationality, education, or a host of other characteristics, but the common denominator is that it is an invasion of an individual's privacy and space and a disregard for a person's desires.

Guidelines for Managers

To ensure zero tolerance of harassment in your department, you have a three-part mandate: be alert, take action, and don't encourage offensive behavior through silence.

Be Alert

At all times, observe what is going on in your department. Don't just look at conditions; be sure you see them. There is a big difference between the two. Looking is passive; it just happens. Seeing is active, and it entails your full attention and participation. Be alert to how staff members behave toward each other and talk to each other. Is there an attitude of cooperation, or is there conflict? If there is conflict, is it directed toward someone because of a perceived difference between that person and others in the group? Is there an "in" group and an "out" group? If so, what determines the "in" and the "out"? Does the "in" group torment members of the "out" group?

If you become aware of anyone's privacy being invaded in any way, be prepared to do something immediately. The sooner you take action, the less arduous the correction will be. Remember, it's a lot easier to extinguish a campfire than a forest fire.

Take Action

Performance reviews, which are the subject of Chapter 12, certainly would be an opportunity to address harassment by an employee, but don't wait until the next scheduled review to take action. Do it right away. The dialogue between you and your staff member must be immediate as well as constructive, and it should support as well as correct. Think of the performance review as a process, not an event, which means that the observations and conversations should be going on all the time.

When you identify what you think is inappropriate behavior, acknowledge it right away to the person responsible; do it privately, and be specific. Specificity is essential because generalities will create hostility and offer little or no chance to correct the situation. State clearly to the offender what was said or done, when, where, to whom, and who else was present. In doing so, you frame and direct the conversation, and you and your employee will be talking about specific actions rather than general interpretations.

When your employee responds to specifics, there can be a succinct discussion that leads to a clear conclusion, but if you allow the discussion to revolve around generalities, only confusion and resentment will result. The situation can then worsen, and you'll have an even bigger problem.

If it is required by your company policy, report the harassment to your supervisor. If a pattern of such behavior develops with an employee over time, this documentation will be important.

Don't Encourage Harassment by Remaining Silent

Part of your job is to promote and protect the welfare of all your employees. If you ever allow, enable, or encourage harassment by remaining silent, there can be at least two serious consequences. One, the situation can get out of hand quickly and become much worse, and two, you may be the one accused of harassment because you let it happen. Both of these consequences can have serious repercussions for you and your company.

There are at least three ways in which you may be alerted to a harassment situation. An employee may complain to you about another employee; you may witness or overhear behaviors that might be considered harassment; and you may see or hear about behavior that you are certain constitutes harassment.

If an employee complains to you about the behavior of another employee, the first thing you must do is listen carefully. Do not offer an opinion, and do not display emotion. Don't react rashly; at this point, all you have is the word of someone who has a vested interest in the charge. Instead, approach the situation by gathering data. Ask specific questions of the person complaining, and then ask specific questions of the person about whom the complaint was made. This is not the time for evaluating the answers but for collecting the information. Inform your supervisor of the situation, and then conduct or cooperate in any subsequent investigation that may take place.

If you observe what may be harassment, ask the employee who was the target of the potential harasser if the behavior was indeed offensive to him or her. If the answer is no, no further action is required on your part. If the answer is yes, explain that such behavior need not be tolerated. Ask questions and conduct an investigation to determine additional facts. Since you thought the behavior might have been offensive, you would be well advised to inform the employee responsible that there might be risks associated with the observed behavior. Do this in a friendly and matter-of-fact manner, not one that would seem to be corrective and accusatory, because the offending employee might not have been aware of the potential reaction to the behavior. An appropriate comment from you at this point could prevent an unpleasant situation in the future.

When you see or hear a behavior that you are certain is harassment, it is your responsibility to stop it right away. Your acknowledgment of the situation and confrontation of the offender may be enough to end the behavior, but you may have to initiate appropriate corrective action to prevent it from happening again. This may include reassigning the offender to another department or shift or, eventually, termination. In any event, you should immediately report the encounter to your supervisor.

Keep a Tight Ship

Regardless of the form it takes, harassment is always about failing to respect others. In order to recognize these behaviors, be attentive to all that goes on around you that might interfere with the privacy of your employees or affront their sensitivities. Collect documentation about accusations of harassment, but don't judge quickly. Keep your management apprised, and if you observe harassment in any form, stop it right away. When your position on harassment is clear to all of your employees, their actions will reflect your model, and that will lead to a safe and productive work environment for everyone.

The following Discovery Lesson will help you practice the skills covered in this chapter and identify these kinds of situations. This all comes back to the differences between looking and seeing, because when you actively observe what is taking place around you, you'll be likely to see situations or problems developing, in time to take appropriate action.

Discovery Lesson

This lesson is an exercise in observation and awareness. It is a chance for you to set your antenna in order to detect something that might be there.

As you move throughout your department, look closely and listen carefully to everything that is taking place. As employees are carrying out their tasks, what else is happening that might impinge on their performance? Look for any indication of an "in" group and an "out" group, and see how members of the latter are treated. Observe what impact that status has on job performance and the climate of the workplace. If there is tension, productivity suffers; if there is mutual support, that spirit of cooperation makes tasks easier for everyone, and that's what you want.

Sometimes language indicates problems. If anyone is being derided, for example, even casually, that might point to future problems. If some employees are "just having some fun" but at the expense of others, that's a strong signal of growing difficulties.

Be conscientious about ensuring that the workplace is comfortable for everyone. If you sense that something might be wrong, get into high gear and address the issue right away. While we hope you don't find any evidence of harassment, it's better to look and not find it than to be surprised later by something you overlooked.

Harassment can be insidious. Offenders might not think they are doing anything wrong, and victims might not feel free to complain. It's your responsibility to be aware of the activities and reactions of both parties. Remember that harassment is not defined by sex, race, age, or other narrow categories; it is about respect. Whether the frequency of harassment complaints has increased because employees are more aware of the behavior or because it has become more prevalent or more visible, you are expected to model proper behavior and to protect those working under your direction. If you are aware, attentive, and responsive, everyone benefits.

Questions to Consider

- *What are you doing to foster a workplace that is comfortable for all of your employees?*

- *Can you identify an "in" group and an "out" group among your employees? If so, what are you doing about it?*

- *Is anyone on your staff excluded from non-work-related social activities? If so, why? Is there anything you can do about it? Is there anything you should do about it?*

Actions speak for themselves. Positive actions say, "I genuinely care"; negative actions say something else. What do your actions say?

11

The Art of Asking Questions

COMMUNICATION IS A VEHICLE THAT ENABLES you and your employees to connect with one another and to learn about your respective worlds. The questions you ask and how you ask them can either strengthen or weaken your connections. Before your employees will feel comfortable sharing information and opinions with you, they must believe they can do so honestly and without retribution. If they feel threatened, they won't share their thoughts, but if they sense that you are willing to listen objectively, they will open up to you.

It's important for you to set the appropriate tone because the way you form and phrase questions will influence how the responses will be presented. This happens because the questions you ask and how you ask them are emblematic of your thoughts, feelings, and attitudes. They can convey such positive messages as:

"I care about you as a person."
"I'm sincerely interested in your ideas."
"I'd like to know so that I can help you solve your problems."
"I'd like to understand you better."
"I need specific information from you."
"I want to help."
"I want to stimulate you to think."
"I want to stimulate a discussion."

Even a manager with the best intentions may ask questions in a way that places employees on the defensive. For example, such questions as "Why do you have such a bad attitude?" or "How many times have I told you not to do that?" are not really questions. They are actually adverse judgmental statements in the form of questions. In these examples, the questioner is not really interested in an answer; the true objective is to chastise or indict the person being addressed.

When you ask the right questions in the right ways, you can learn much from your employees. You can find out what's happening and why. You can gain valuable information and insights to help you function better in your job. You can also learn about what your employees are thinking, what turns them on, what turns them off, what upsets them, what stimulates them, and more.

In your role as manager, a primary task is to get your staff to contribute and participate. Communication is a two-way road. Before you can accurately direct your staff, you must understand the people you are directing, and you do that by asking. It takes a few additional minutes out of your busy day, but it will save a great deal of time over the long haul.

Have a Clear Destination

Fundamental to the art of asking the right questions is knowing exactly what you are looking for. When you have a firm idea of what you need, write it down. This gives you a focus and destination, analogous to your preparation before taking a road trip. If you've planned the journey and you know your destination, you'll get there. Even if you have to take a detour, you will get to where you want to go. Without a clear-cut destination, you can drive for a long time and use a lot of fuel but not end up in the place you really want to be. It may be fun to do that, and it can be an interesting diversion, but it won't accomplish your intended mission.

You can always make time for fun if you want to, but the purpose of this chapter is to help you stay on track and reach your goals. Those goals must be apparent to all parties, and your staff will follow your lead. Unless you're simply making small talk, when you're asking your employees business-related questions, have a definite destination in mind. Don't allow yourself to stray from your course.

You may be thinking, "Everyone asks questions all the time. What's new here?" Although it's true that people habitually ask questions, often those questions are posed with no plan and without forethought to the reaction they might elicit. Here's a simple example of how the question determines the answer: If you ask someone to describe the biggest problems he or she faces at work, you'll get a list of problems. If, on the other hand, you ask about that person's greatest opportunities, you will get a much different listing. You get what you ask for, so be careful how you ask.

As further illustration, the following scene was played out recently in a department store:

A woman and her young daughter, probably eight or nine years old, were shopping for a dress for the child. The mother gestured to a rack of dresses and asked, "Which dress do you want?"

The little girl smiled and pointed to her choice. "This one."

"Oh, that wouldn't look good on you," said the mother. "The color and style are all wrong for you."

"But I like it. I think it's nice."

The mother picked up another dress. "How about this one?"

"I don't like that one. I like the one I picked out."

In the end, the little girl was in tears, her mother was angry with her, and no dress was purchased that day.

What went wrong? The mother asked the wrong question. She asked her daughter to make a selection from a wide variety of choices. The mother established a broad, unrestricted range despite the fact that she had already imposed certain limitations herself regarding color and style. She asked a question, and she prompted the child to make a selection. When the child complied, the mother rejected her decision.

There probably would have been little turmoil if the mother had established a different sequence of events. Since she knew what her acceptable range of choices included, she could have selected three or four dresses that met her criteria and then asked, "Which one of these pretty dresses would you like?"

Whichever of those dresses the little girl picked would have been acceptable to the mother, and the daughter would have been happy with her choice. It was her decision, after all. Mother also would have been happy because she had provided guidance and direction. It would have been one of those win-win situations rather than a disaster, because the framing of the question often dictates the outcome.

Techniques You Can Use to Your Advantage

You have a variety of methods at your disposal to gather and exchange information. The following sections outline five techniques for results-oriented communication: closed questions, open questions, probing questions, echoes, and follow-up questions.

Closed Questions

Closed questions produce short, usually one-word answers and do not leave much room for discussion. This category includes queries that begin with "Can," "Do," "Is," "Will," "When," "Who," and "Did." Note the ways such closed questions can be answered:

Question Beginning with	Typical Answer
Can	Yes or No
Do	Yes or No
Is	Yes or No
Will	Yes, No, or Maybe
When	Tuesday
Who	Charlie
Did	Yes or No

Closed questions are useful when you want to confirm information or when you want a straightforward answer, with no elaboration, to a straightforward question. These kinds of questions do not engender discussion. Furthermore, they might even hinder a free exchange of information because they often seem to be an interrogation.

Frequently, simple answers such as these are not satisfactory because you are looking for explanations, reasons, and examples. When you've used closed questions with your subordinates, you probably noticed that your questions were a lot longer than their answers. This means that you are working harder and talking more than the employee you're addressing. Think for a moment about this difference in length between the question and the answer. Since you are asking a question to get information, the person of whom you're asking the question must be persuaded or encouraged to share that information. Closed questions will yield only minimum information. To gain more information, you must get your employee to talk more than you. By employing open questions, you increase your chances of accomplishing that objective.

Open Questions

Open questions usually start with "How," "What," and "Why." These formats require lengthier responses than closed questions. No matter how hard someone tries, these questions cannot be satisfactorily answered with one word.

Crafting open questions requires more attention than phrasing closed questions. Once you say the first word, you have to figure out what the rest of the sentence will be. You have to identify your area of interest and focus.

"How will _____ ?"

"What _____ ?"

"Why _____ ?"

You must tread carefully with such questions because, as has been demonstrated, the way you ask them will usually preprogram the answer. It will stake out the territory for exploration, and your employee will just follow your lead. For example, if you were to ask someone, "What is the toughest challenge you have to overcome?" it's logical for the person to tell you how he or she views the challenge and plans to deal with it. Then again, if you were to ask, "What do you need from me to meet your current challenge?" you may find yourself more involved in this person's caseload than you care to be. Open questions can be valuable; just remember to construct them so that you ask for what you really want to know.

"Why" questions are especially tricky. While they are as legitimate as others, you have to be particularly cognizant of how they might be perceived by your employee. This form of question can do much more than ask for reasons. It can be interpreted as a request for information, or as accusatory and entrapping. For example, here is a why question that, clearly, simply seeks information: "I was wondering, why did you choose option X rather than Y?" It may, however, sound judgemental: "Why would you do such a foolish thing?"

Don't ask "why" when there is nothing the responder could say that would be acceptable to you. Those are trap questions, which place the person on the defensive. For example: "Why did you submit this sloppy report?" or "Why did you buy such an ugly tie?" No answer to either of those shots would satisfy the questioner. There is no way the responder can win or can infer that the questioner really wants information. Such questions are obviously accusatory. Here again, you can see how the framing of the question determines the answer.

Probing Questions

Probing questions dig more deeply into an area already established by either a closed or an open question. They prod responders to talk about what is important to them. The objective of using probes is to obtain additional detail about the subject being presented to you. When you use either an open or a closed question, it is you who identifies the area for discussion. An appropriate question of either type will prime the pump; information will start to flow, but it might stop abruptly. There is an easy way to keep it flowing, and you don't have to work hard to think up new questions. All you have to do is call on a short list of standards that will fit almost any situation. Try these:

> "What gives you that impression?"
> "What makes you say that?"
> "Really?"
> "Would you elaborate?"
> "Would you give me an example?"
> "What else should I know?"
> "Why do you say that?"
> "Tell me more."

This format can fit any situation, regardless of the topic. Probes such as these keep the conversation moving. Moreover, the responders are invited to select the areas that are important to them. As you hear what aspect responders select and what they add, you develop greater insight into what is important to them. In fact, people who are adept at using this technique are regarded as great conversationalists because they can keep others talking.

You'll have many occasions to use probes in your managerial career. For instance, suppose you are interviewing someone for a job. In response to one of your questions, the applicant says, "I have good communication skills." You might probe by asking, "What kind of communication skills are you referring to?" Or, if an employee says, "I'm having trouble with Frankie," you might ask, "Will you elaborate?" The benefit is that you quickly find out what you need to know without working hard.

Echoes

Probes can also take the form of an echo, a technique in which you repeat a few of the responder's words back to the person. In almost every instance, the responder will keep talking. It's that simple.

Suppose a person says, "I'm having a tough time with this assignment." You respond, "A tough time?" Or, a disgruntled employee says, "It's unfair that I get blamed for everything that goes wrong around here." Your echo might be, "Everything?" or "Get blamed?" The echo says in effect, "I heard you, and you are invited to continue telling me whatever you want to tell me."

Echoes are a handy tool for probing when a person talks in generalizations or abstractions. Try it the next time someone falls back on a generalization when talking to you. All you have to do is echo, "Always?" or "Never?" See how it works in response to generalizations such as "John's attitude is terrible." or "Mary is so irresponsible." Just say, "Terrible?" or "Irresponsible?" You'll probably get more information than you ever expected. Another reliable alternative is to reply, "Tell me more." Then, stand back because the new information will come in waves.

Follow-Up Questions

This last technique is a variation of the first three, but it is used to gather data, evidence, and support of an initial comment. Here, you are following up on something the person said to round out your information on the subject in which you're interested. For example, "Earlier you said, _____. I'd like to discuss this in a little more detail."

That sentence, "Earlier you said, _____," does something else for you and your staff: it demonstrates that you listened. When you communicate that to your staff, you also demonstrate that you value them; you value what they have to say, and you want them to tell you more.

This harks back to Chapter 5 and the value of listening. Once you ask a question, be ready to be an active listener. Here is a guiding rule: If you don't plan to listen to the answer, don't ask the question! You'll just be wasting everyone's time.

Ask Questions in the Right Way

All of the five major questioning techniques described are useful, but they won't work well unless you ask your questions in the right ways. Make certain your attitudes are positive and your intentions are honorable, so that the person with whom you're talking interprets what you say as you intended.

The first priority is to make eye contact. Look right at the other party, both when you talk and when you listen. If eye contact falters, trust and confidence diminish. When you look at your employees, it demonstrates that you value them. During the time you are communicating with them, they should feel that they are the focal point of your world. A bonus is that, if you give undivided attention to them, you will likely receive it from them in return.

Second, take notes. It is often appropriate to record key points of your talks with staff members. Again, when you write down people's words, you demonstrate that you value the comments—and the speaker. Be sure to accompany your note taking with an explanation such as "That's important" or "I didn't know that." You want to convey that your intention is to capture the words because they are pertinent and not because you are gathering evidence that could be used against the person.

When you ask questions, you know that your intentions are honorable, but be sure you communicate that honor by what you do and how you do it. If your attitude is perceived as negative or if your behavior is interpreted as confrontational, you can expect a defensive reaction. Once that happens, you have conflict rather than effective communication.

Confirm, Clarify, or Expand

Asking the right questions in the right ways will put you in close touch with your employees. The right way will depend on your intentions, so be sure of what you want to do: do you want to confirm, clarify, or expand?

When you want to confirm information, closed questions might be your best choice because you'll generally get "yes" or "no" responses. You'll get the short answers that can lead you to specific action or agreement.

When you want to clarify, the open question will produce the details you need to fully understand the response. Open questions enable you to seek additional data in areas you feel are important.

When you want to expand, use the probes, echoes, and follow-up questions that allow and encourage answers that reflect the responder's interests and priorities. Once you identify what is important to the person, follow that lead, and the person will keep talking.

Use these five techniques when you're asking questions. Know what you want, and choose the course that will lead you to your destination. Know exactly where you want to go and what you want to learn.

When you're asking questions, view yourself as the student of the person you're questioning. And remember: You don't learn much when you are talking. So, when you ask questions, silence is golden. Listen—really listen. Remember also that there's a good reason we each have two ears but only one mouth. Listen more than you talk when you want to gather information. If we talk too much, we might set up barriers and not get what we want. Good communication keeps the traffic flowing in both directions.

Practice, Practice, Practice

Asking the right questions in the right ways does not come naturally to most of us. To become comfortable with these techniques, practice them whenever you talk with your neighbors, your family, or your spouse. Practice them with everyone. Don't wait to use the questioning techniques until you are face-to-face with a recalcitrant staff member.

Just as with any sport you might play, you practice the skills over and over before you get into a game. That way, in the pressure of competition, you will use the skills automatically. You won't have to think your way through a behavior if you have made it a natural part of yourself. So, practice, practice, and practice some more—on your children, in social settings, anytime you have the opening.

You don't have to juggle all of the techniques right away or at the same time. Pick one or two that feel comfortable, and work with only them until you can easily see their application and the results they can produce, and then try the others. Soon you'll be using all of them with regularity, and you'll be pleased with what you accomplish.

Discovery Lesson

Try out some or all of the five questioning techniques the next time you're at a dinner party. No one will know what you are doing as long as you remember to engage in the conversation rather than merely lob a battery of questions. Your fellow diners won't be aware of anything out of the ordinary. They will respond and participate.

You'll probably discover that you are drawing out people who had previously been quiet. By using the techniques you've learned, you will involve others in the conversation. You'll be impressed by how easily the conversations unfold.

This tactic works because it gets the other people to talk about what is important to them. We all love to talk about our own interests, and your efforts will facilitate that process.

Once you've developed the skill of asking the right questions in the right ways, you'll be surprised at how much you will learn and grow professionally—and personally. When you practice and hone these questioning skills, you become an accomplished conversationalist, lauded in a variety of situations. When you demonstrate interest in others, they will open up to you. When you demonstrate that you value people's ideas, they will share them with you. And when your staff members share their ideas, you have more data with which to make your management decisions.

These are basic techniques that you can modify once you have mastered them. Imprint your own style, of course, but use them, and see what happens.

Questions to Consider

- *How can I best discover what is of most interest to my employees?*

- *When I need to develop a new way of accomplishing a task, how can I collect the necessary data? What should I look for?*

- *Within the next week, what opportunities will allow me to put these targeted ways of asking questions to good use?*

12

Conduct Meaningful Performance Reviews

THE PREVIOUS CHAPTER DESCRIBED A SET of methods for collecting information. This chapter concerns why you should collect it and what you will do with the information. Finding out about your employees and their work habits is important because eventually you will have to conduct a formal performance review with each of them, and the more information you have, the more valuable those reviews will be. Many managers don't like to give performance reviews because they are uncomfortable with the process, and they don't want to appear to be checking up on their employees.

Noting progress, however, is practical whether you're taking a road trip, going on a diet, or cheering for the home team. With each of those activities, you check the progress almost as a matter of habit, and you probably don't think much about the process. You know the value to be gained from charting advancement.

As a manager, one of your primary responsibilities is monitoring progress within your department. Are you meeting quotas? Is production on schedule? Has inventory been consistent? There are usually corporate timetables and forms to assist in these progress checks. You use them because it is essential for you to know what is going on in your department, and they are probably required by your upper management. Fortified with such information, you can take action to correct where necessary, modify where appropriate, or reinforce where beneficial.

To do this effectively with your employees, you need a plan, and you need a timetable. Scheduled performance reviews are like any other progress check, but they pertain to people rather than activities. Managers sometimes are reluctant to conduct these reviews because the conversations are so personal, and if they are not done well, they can lead to hurt feelings or morale problems.

The Importance of Performance Reviews

Performance reviews are essential for developing your employees. They are also valuable to you. When the reviews are done correctly, your employees will learn how they are doing, what they should be doing differently, what their strengths are, what their weaknesses are, how they can improve, and what help they need to reach their full potential. You, in turn, learn what you must do to help them progress.

You need to provide guidance and direction to your employees. You have the vantage point, and you must be sure that your employees understand their roles in accomplishing departmental goals. In this sense, you are like the captain of a ship. You know the destination and the route, but you must rely on your crew to do what is necessary to get the ship safely to port. You can't do it alone! Sailing is a team effort, and everyone has an important task. The captain needs all members of the crew to perform in a manner that will lead everyone on board to the desired destination.

Therefore, you must know your employees, their levels of performance, and what each needs to reach port. Conducting a beneficial performance review will help you obtain that information. As with so many other areas of your job, you need a plan before you can begin.

For starters, to conduct a meaningful performance review, you must be clear about what you want to accomplish. Do you want to praise the employee? Set the employee straight? Tell the employee what he or she did well? Tell the employee what he or she did poorly? Tell the employee what has to be fixed? Agree on what the employee has to do? Agree on how the employee can accomplish certain objectives?

There are elements of all of these communications in most performance reviews.

The Performance Review Should Be a Process, Not an Event

If you do your job correctly, there will be sufficient ongoing communication so that all your employees know what is expected of them and how well or poorly they are doing. That way, when the formal review date arrives and the discussions begin, there will be no bolts from the blue.

That's the way it should be, but not every manager lives up to this standard. In the following anecdote, the manager, Mike, thought he was doing well; he thought he was delegating, but his method and his intervention didn't lead to a productive outcome.

Mike said to his employee, Jake, after he was hired, "I describe my style of management as the Vacuum Theory of Management." When Jake asked what that was, Mike said, "As long as everything is going well, you won't hear from me, but the minute something goes wrong, I'll be all over you like a tent."

If Jake had heard that before he had accepted the position, his decision might have been different. Perhaps he didn't ask the right questions during his interview; if he had, he might have realized that this approach would not be conducive to his professional development.

As it was, every time Mike came into Jake's office or even walked toward him, Jake's first thought was, "What have I done wrong?"

Mike thought silence was delegation and support. That silence, though, caused everyone else to wonder, "Am I doing OK? I haven't heard from him lately."

Preparing for the formal performance review with Mike was like getting ready to testify before a congressional committee. The event was tense because the manager was clearly in control and obviously liked it that way. The review was a report card on past activities; he was the parent, and every employee was his child. Those reviews simply didn't work and were not effective two-way communications.

Though Jake was an able producer, and both he and the organization had made a substantial investment of time in his training, he soon resigned. Eventually, many others in the department were as disgruntled as Jake was by the Vacuum Theory of Management, and they too left.

Mike continued to hire new people, evaluate them, and eventually watch them leave. That cycle was both expensive and time-consuming, and it certainly didn't contribute to the long-term profitability of the company.

Recall from previous chapters the image of the master gardener tending a garden. Note the word *tend*, which means "to take care of, to minister to, to watch over, to look after."

The gardener pays attention to the garden all the time. This includes tilling the soil, watering it as appropriate, and fertilizing it regularly. It's more than just selecting and planting seeds and then looking in on them every once in a while, because gardening is a continuous nurturing process. Similarly, as manager of your department, you must be attentive to your employees—all the time.

Another way to look at the process-versus-event concept and the need to be continually alert is to compare it to driving a car. At the wheel, you are constantly observing traffic, pedestrians, and signs; measuring your location, your relation to other objects, and your speed; and making adjustments as necessary—slowing down, speeding up, changing lanes. You also watch the gauges to monitor fuel consumption, temperature, electrical power, pressure, and other indicators of how well or poorly your vehicle is running. You don't wait until the end of the trip to check these items to see how you did. That would incur the risk of not completing the trip. So, you check constantly to see how you are doing. At the wheel of your department, you monitor similar indicators with regard to your employees.

Six Steps for Productive Performance Reviews

Let's assume that you and the members of your staff are engaged in ongoing communication. You are now conducting a formal annual performance review with one of your employees, and you want it to be productive. You and he had previously agreed on specific goals and expectations that you're now reviewing.

This section takes you through the appropriate steps.

1. Identify what the employee has done well and what he has done poorly during the past year by citing specific positive and negative behaviors.

   The key word here is *specific*, because when you establish the area of discussion, you set the focus. When you concentrate on specific actions, both you and your employee will be discussing the same thing.

   For example, if lateness is identified as a problem, a specific comment might be, "In the past two weeks, you have punched in at least twenty minutes late on four occasions." There is no question about those details. Now consider this opening sentence: "You've been coming in late a lot recently." Definitions are needed here in order to deduce how late is *late*, what constitutes *a lot*, and when is *recently*.

   When you begin the review, be sure that you and your employee are looking at the situation in the same way. Don't use vague words because they will only lead to vague discussions, and vague discussions usually lead to misunderstandings.

Be equally specific in commenting on positive actions, which should also be included in the review. A frequently heard comment in the workplace and elsewhere is "Good job." What does that mean? No one knows for sure because it's such a vague statement. Consider how much more of an impact the following statement makes because it is more precise: "You reduced expenses by 12 percent over the last month. Well done."

Here is a simple rule for achieving a direct, productive conversation during a performance review: Because the actions of an employee led you to a particular conclusion, when you begin the discussion, try to focus on the actions rather than on your conclusions.

2. Encourage dialogue, and then listen to the reactions and explanations.

Give the employee the opportunity to describe things as he sees them, while you listen, and then respond appropriately. Once you have established the specifics of the discussion and have described your observations, stop talking. The employee will likely have a reaction, so listen to it. He may agree, he may correct, or he may want to expand. All of these responses are good because they all keep the dialogue engaged. Your task here is to continue to move ahead in order to improve his performance.

In addition to searching for facts, watch and listen for signals about emotions the employee might display. Is he shifting in his chair? Are his eyes darting around the room? Is he stumbling over his words? These signs will help you understand how the employee is reacting to your comments, and that understanding will contribute to a meaningful review. If you gain insight on how the employee feels, you'll be better able to understand what he does. Ask appropriate questions to keep the dialogue going. (Review Chapter 11 for techniques of asking questions.)

3. Discuss the implications of changing or not changing negative behaviors.

Explain what will happen if the employee continues to underperform as stated. Describe the consequences in detail. For example: "I'll have to put you on probation for two months" or "You won't be eligible for the transfer until you are on time on a regular basis." By being specific, you will not appear to be casting idle threats with unfair generalizations.

Also use appropriate positive comments: "You're due for a promotion within the next quarter," or "There is a raise coming effective your next pay period," or "You are on target for a bonus this year." This will give the employee the incentive to improve.

While positive language is more likely to elicit change, if the situation requires that you warn the employee about the penalties for continued negative behavior, be sure that the employee knows exactly where he stands. Conveying the truth and clearing the air will contribute to a better working relationship. Be sure, however, that this clarity is connected to future actions and improvements that will benefit the company and the employee's satisfaction and performance. This leads to the next step.

4. Link past accomplishments to whatever changes are needed.

For example, if the person was good with inventory in a prior assignment, show him how those same detail skills could help him make specific improvements that you are seeking in order processing. Make sure the employee knows how the strength or skill he has demonstrated relates to what is expected of him in the future. Then help him understand how to make the necessary changes.

5. Agree on an action plan.

Together, develop a plan for changing unacceptable behaviors to acceptable ones and for continuing behaviors that are positive. As the two of you develop this plan, put the major responsibility for suggesting the actions squarely on the shoulders of the employee. To accomplish this, use the word *you* when phrasing your questions. For example:

"What can you do to _____?"
"What ideas do you have for _____?"
"What suggestions do you have to _____?"

This simple technique encourages the employee to take responsibility for planning the course of action required to reach his destination. It's a powerful tactic because people are more likely to follow through on their own ideas than on what they are told to do by someone else.

If you impose the solution on the employee, you might garner his agreement at the moment, but there may be little or no follow-through, and a prime opportunity will have been lost. Your goal is to extract a long-term commitment from your employee to modify his behavior, not just to placate him temporarily.

6. Follow up.

Agree on when you will meet again and what specific behaviors, actions, and attitudes you will review. When there is a clear understanding of what's expected, and a clear plan for achieving it, future measurements and evaluations are easier and employees will become more productive.

Everyone Wins

Adhering to the foregoing six steps will make discussions of performance meaningful to your staff and to you. In fact, how well you conduct your reviews with your employees may be one of the skills on which you are evaluated during your own reviews. Thus, applying these steps can contribute to a positive report on your performance review while you are helping your employees improve. With this process, everyone wins.

Conducting an effective performance review is not only good business but also the right thing to do. Your employees deserve to know how you rate their progress, so praising as well as correcting is appropriate. The most important concept to remember is that worthwhile performance reviews are the results of ongoing assessments and corrections. There should be no surprises in the formal review. And it should be a pleasant learning and planning experience for both you and your employees.

Questions to Consider

- *What do I need to know about each employee before setting up the formal performance review?*

- *For each employee, what should I look for during the session that will tell me if I'm getting through? What signals might employees be sending?*

- *If I'm going to meet with everyone on my staff, how much time can I allocate for each review? Where can I carve that time out of my schedule?*

As a manager, you are entitled to certain powers. How wisely you exercise these powers determines your effectiveness.

13

Make Departmental Meetings Productive

HAVE YOU EVER BEEN TO A MEETING that was too short and too productive? Didn't think so. Though short and productive is what participants strive for, most business meetings are just the opposite. The reasons for this state of affairs are numerous. This chapter sheds light on a few of the more salient ones to help prepare you for the many meetings you'll be running in the course of your career.

Compare the hits and misses that you read about here with your own experiences at meetings that you have attended and found to be productive or tedious or somewhere in between. Use these reactions as a basic indicator of how your employees are going to feel about the meetings you conduct. Presumably, you want to run meetings that won't cause your employees to groan when one is announced. Avoid that fate by learning both what causes bad, unproductive meetings and how you can make yours good, productive ones.

Many meetings are held just because they are on a regular schedule. For example, at 10:00 A.M. every Monday, there is a staff meeting. Is the meeting being held because it is important and necessary, or because it is Monday morning and it's expected to occur? All too often, it's the latter. When everyone on the staff plans to go to a meeting because it's on a schedule, someone has to decide what to talk about. An agenda is then manufactured to justify the meeting.

This backward process is an application of Parkinson's law (C. Northcote Parkinson, a notable British economist), which states: "Every job can be expanded to fill the amount of time allotted to it." If a one-hour period is scheduled for a meeting, the meeting will usually last an hour—or perhaps a little more. If it's two hours on the schedule, then that's how long the meeting will last.

A successful manager conducts a meeting only because it is necessary and not because it is habit. When you and your employees are occupied at a meeting, the functional tasks for which you are responsible are not being performed. They will be taken care of sometime, of course, but they now have to be fit into the time remaining after the meeting rather than within the full workday. This is why short, concise, and productive meetings are so important. The point is not that meetings are bad; it's that they should be carried out using a plan.

Plan Your Meetings

Whether you are conducting an international satellite meeting incorporating hundreds of locations or addressing a small staff in your conference room, you must take a few key actions to ensure that the meeting yields maximum value. If you are like many people we know, a scant few departmental meetings that you've attended were as productive as you would have liked. Now that you're in charge, you have the power to optimize your meetings.

The keys are to use your time well, foster healthy communication among participants, and make sure the purposes of your meetings were fulfilled.

Use Everyone's Time Well— It's Expensive

Time is a nonrenewable commodity; when it's gone, it's gone. You can't put unused time in a plastic bag, place it in the refrigerator, and have it tomorrow as a leftover if you don't make the most of it today. To use time well, you have to plan each meeting. You also have to sharpen your time-management skills. The planning starts by answering the following questions and committing those answers to writing:

- Why am I holding this meeting?
- Who will be there? Why?
- Who will do what on the agenda?
- How long will it take?
- What specifically do I want to accomplish?

Why am I holding this meeting?

Many reasons—valid or otherwise—are cited for holding meetings, including because it's Friday and we meet every Friday; a situation must be addressed; or a new procedure must be explained. Always have a clear and definite reason for holding a meeting, and inform everyone involved what the reason is.

Don't automatically assume that assembling as a group is the most practical format for your purpose. If face-to-face contact isn't necessary, maybe a simple memo will serve instead. Today's workplace puts a wide variety of communication techniques at people's fingertips. To decide which to use for a given occasion, compare their relative merits. For instance, face-to-face interactions may be necessary in order to share materials and elicit immediate feedback. E-mail or conference calls might be a better way to go if you need people's ideas but not their physical presence. A questionnaire could be the most efficient and least threatening way of securing widespread participation, since people can respond from the relative safety of their offices or homes. Having determined what is required and what is available, use the technique that is justified by the task at hand.

Who will be there? Why?

If the whole department is required to attend, you have to ask yourself who is minding the store. If only selected individuals are required to attend, decide who, as well as how will they be notified. In such cases, in the spirit of goodwill and information sharing, you may want to inform the other members of the department why they were not invited.

If there will be guests, who are they and what will their roles be? Will your staff be told in advance, and if so, how? Decide what method you will use to ensure that complete information is available to all parties.

Who will do what on the agenda?

Designate the people who will be called on to give a presentation and what they will be expected to do. Since you want constructive input, you must enable the speakers to prepare by giving them sufficient advance information. Everyone expected to attend is entitled to have enough foundation and time to prepare and then contribute. By making your goals known sufficiently in advance, you will produce a more orderly and productive session.

Staff members should be able to suggest agenda items too, but this should be done well in advance of the meeting so that you are able to review the additions and make changes, if necessary. Surprise agenda items often contribute heat but little light to a meeting.

How long will it last?

Inform everyone who'll be attending of both the start time and end time. This, too, is a matter of respect. Everyone's time is valuable, not just yours, so be sure you demonstrate your recognition of that value.

Build an agenda carefully, and stay with it. Ask prospective attendees what issues they would like brought up so you can include them as appropriate. If a suggestion doesn't fit the current agenda and is not urgent, put it on a future agenda. Allocate a time limit for each item to be covered, and plan how you'll keep track of the time from the very start of the meeting. If conditions require, you can always add time to a particular item by subtracting an equal amount from another item or by postponing the other item until the next meeting.

Print the agenda and distribute copies to all participants—prior to the meeting whenever possible but certainly no later than the start of the meeting. Have extra copies available for any unexpected attendees. If you delegate any part of this task to an employee, be sure the person understands the importance of a concise and readily available agenda.

What specifically do I want to accomplish?

At the end of the meeting, how will you know that your objectives were achieved? This is perhaps the most pertinent question. If you can't answer it clearly and quickly, you might want to reconsider holding the meeting until you have a definable goal.

A large food and drug retailer found itself in this type of fix. The company's upper management concluded that the meetings they were holding were unproductive and expensive. Here's how they used to do it:

They met every Monday at 1:00 P.M. and would work all the way through every agenda item—an undertaking that, at times, took in excess of two hours to complete. To complicate matters, the meetings were conducted over the company's dedicated television system. The principal players were in a TV studio with two-way telephone connections to the receiving locations at a score of stores across the United States. The people in the studio talked at, not with, the people in the stores. They described products, promotions, and procedures that headquarters determined were most important. The viewers sat in designated rooms at each location and listened to these descriptions. At the end of the presentations, viewers could ask questions over the telephone lines.

Management described the process as "OK but boring and expensive." The "OK" comment pertained to the perceived value of the material; "boring" referred to the performance of the presenters; and "expensive" applied not only to the cost of the equipment but also to the time expended by all the viewers who were taken away from their jobs to watch the meeting in progress.

Lost productivity, like lost time, can never be regained. The solution lies in changing what doesn't work.

Provide a Reason for the Meeting

Streamlining the meeting process just depicted made the sessions more productive and less of a chore for participants. You can apply these same principles, distilled from the five questions in the preceding section, to make the most of your meetings.

1. *Scheduling:* The scheduling of future meetings was based on the need for them and on the material requiring coverage—not on the fact that it was Monday. Some weeks, there were no meetings, and no one ever registered a complaint about that.

2. *Attendees:* Only people who were directly influenced by and related to the content had to attend. The department was covered at all times, and productivity continued.

3. *Participants:* All participants were contacted well in advance and briefed on what had to be covered, why, and within what time frame. That time frame was rarely altered.

4. *Time:* Often the participants took less time than was allocated but never more. They had a framework and stayed with it. They were never denounced for conducting a meeting that was too short.

5. *Goals:* Before presenting, all scheduled speakers wrote out their goals and how they intended to accomplish them. This activity required full participation. As you plan your own meetings, think about how you can encourage your attendees to map their goals. Use the discipline of the blank piece of paper: If you can't write out your goals succinctly, you probably won't meet them, and if you don't achieve your goals, then your meeting accomplished nothing.

In addition to these changes, all participants were required to attend an instructional session to learn how to make effective presentations on TV and in face-to-face situations. The techniques and skills of giving presentations are often overlooked in professional development. Most managers concentrate on control, and they ignore how that control is packaged and delivered. However, audiences—and employees—respond to the packaging and the delivery more than they do to the control.

If you have not already done so, do yourself and your employees a favor and sign yourself up for a presentation techniques class. You'll be impressed by how useful those tools are. While you probably won't be holding media-based meetings right away, the basic principles are essentially the same for every meeting you run. Simply put: plan, then execute.

Foster Healthy Communication Among Your Staff

A meeting is an opportunity for a group of people to come together to share ideas. The extent of sharing runs the gamut from a "show and tell" by an individual to full and open dialogue by all in attendance. There will be many times when you must provide your staff with information, and you have many ways to do so. No matter how you choose to dispense information, allow and encourage participation as frequently as possible. Regularly seek out new and fresh ideas from your employees. When you have all the possible information available, you can avoid mistakes that might hinder your progress as a manager.

A recent survey of managers asked: What are the biggest mistakes managers make? As you read through this sampling of their responses, consider how you can avoid these errors in meetings you conduct. They cited these attributes of a poor manager:

- Assumes he or she knows what the problem is
- Assumes employees are as enthusiastic as he or she is
- Has all the answers
- Doesn't know what else is going on in employees' lives
- Frequently doesn't know what the real problems are
- Talks too much and frequently doesn't listen
- Doesn't seem to care what employees think or feel
- Doesn't encourage feedback
- Corrects more than praises

Have you or other managers you know ever made these mistakes? By avoiding these pitfalls, you will demonstrate to your employees how to conduct themselves in a meeting. Modeling professional behavior is much stronger and clearer than words.

Make Sure the Purposes of Your Meeting Are Fulfilled

To help guarantee that the effort will be productive and informative, always provide people attending with advance notice of the precise nature of the meeting. Before the session gets under way, or in the previously distributed agenda, spell out what you plan to accomplish. This enables everyone to get organized and helps keep the proceedings on target and on track. All members of the group will be better equipped to participate in both the discussions and the solutions, and that compounded strength will be a resource for you and them.

Before you end, ask for a consensus on whether the specified objectives have been achieved. If they have not, identify what remains and when it can be completed. Think this one through. In some cases, you'll find that it makes sense to remand the unfinished business for discussions outside the particular group gathered. Be careful not to place unnecessary demands on others' time.

The department meeting is an opportunity for you and your staff to join together to examine and resolve issues to the benefit of all concerned. So:

- Plan your meetings—in writing.
- Strive for the broadest participation possible.
- Make sure everyone agrees that your objectives were met.

Use the Discovery Lesson to test out some of the ideas in this chapter. To gain maximum benefit, put what you learn into practice so that these behaviors become a natural part of your management style.

Discovery Lesson

Next time you attend a meeting as a participant, note what was good about the meeting and what was not. Did you observe a particular technique or action that you could implement to advantage in your own meetings?

This change in perspective can pay dividends in your efforts to plan and execute the meetings that are your responsibility. For most of us, it is always easier to see the shortcomings in what others do than in what we do ourselves. If you pay close attention to how others are running meetings, you'll accrue a wide range of ideas about what works and what doesn't.

The principles in this chapter are almost universal, although certain variations may apply to your organization or industry. Keep looking for ways to improve on your meetings and internal communications. These observations will lead you to insights and behavior changes that will profit your department and, ultimately, your company. Remember to always be a student, and keep learning.

Questions to Consider

- *Why do I hold meetings in the first place?*

- *Whom do I expect and/or require to attend? What is their function at the meetings, and what do they have to contribute?*

- *How can I best use meeting time: To give reports? To ask questions? Other?*

Outstanding managers are like accomplished and respected directors. They make their presence felt without being obvious about their influence.

Excellent managers increase the value of the people reporting to them.

14

Delegate Effectively and Allow Employees to Take Risks

IT IS HUMAN NATURE TO DO those things with which we are most comfortable and to avoid what makes us uncomfortable. Usually, that comfort level comes either from our experiences with a situation or from the guidance and support of someone else.

Your employees can provide you with assistance if they feel free to make suggestions and are comfortable in exploring new options. Taking those chances, however, can be a bit frightening for some of them. A large part of your job is to motivate others to take on new responsibilities and to grow and excel in their jobs.

This chapter shows you how to encourage employees to take risks and how you can best delegate responsibilities. If you are adept at delegating, your employees will feel safe and will be receptive to taking on additional duties. This precept is at the very heart of being a manager. You can't to do everything yourself, and you shouldn't try. Instead, you must motivate other people to do things and to do them well.

This is easily said but sometimes a feat to pull off. Employees may be overly accustomed to doing a specific job in a certain way; giving them a new task or a new format for accomplishing that task might require a change in methodology that is uncomfortable. When you assign a task, you aren't giving up responsibility for it but rather allowing another to carry out the task instead of doing it yourself. Yes, it's uncomfortable for both parties, but it works when done right, and it's the cornerstone of all businesses.

You can give your employees the incentive to try change and to take risks if you set up the appropriate conditions. Employees are likely to feel safe when you provide a safety net for them, when the risks you ask them to take are reasonable, and when the assigned duties fit their level of ability. Your job is to observe, guide, and protect the risk takers.

Delegation in Action

Here's an instructive account of how, by delegating well, an authority figure allowed someone he valued and trusted to take a reasonable risk. Although that someone was his daughter, the principles he employed in this personal situation also apply to business.

Larry's sixteen-year-old daughter, Susan, had just passed her driver's test and received her license. Several weeks later, the family decided to take a short road trip to visit relatives in a neighboring state. Susan asked if she could plan the trip and, of course, do the driving. After Larry and his wife gave their permission, Susan went to work on her plan. She got out the maps, checked the possible routes, and finally settled on the best (the fastest) option. Larry could have told her what it was, but this was her trip and her plan.

When the day of embarkation arrived, Susan slid behind the wheel, Larry's wife sat in the front passenger's seat, and Larry settled into the backseat with a newspaper. Susan started the car, and they were on their way.

Larry made a big show of reading the newspaper as though he weren't watching where they were going. In time, he noticed that Susan was going a bit too fast and was in the wrong lane to exit onto another road. It was obvious to him that she was going to miss the turnoff.

Larry had a dilemma. Should he tell her and prevent her making a mistake, or should he bite his tongue and let her commit the error? He had delegated planning the trip to her. If he were to jump in and correct her, he would be removing the delegation and communicating a message that she was incapable of executing her task. If, on the other hand, he remained quiet, she would miss the turn, and that would add to the length of the trip.

It was a test of his mettle for Larry to sit quietly and watch as Susan sailed past the exit. In about fifteen minutes (it seemed hours to him) she announced, "Something is wrong."

"Oh?" said Larry. "What?"

She pulled over to the side of the road, stopped, and unfolded the map. "I missed the turnoff," she said, "but we can turn around right up the road and get back to the exit in a flash." And that's what she did.

The lesson is clear. Larry let Susan take a reasonable risk. Sure, she made a mistake, but they ended up where they planned to go. It took a little longer, but that was of no real importance because Susan gained some knowledge that day.

Larry acknowledged afterward that his composure during the incident required courage. "Perhaps it also required a risk on my part," he said. "But I was just being a good father. I helped her to grow a little."

A main function of managers is to help their employees grow professionally. Encouraging them to take reasonable risks is a good way of performing that function.

Simply defined, a risk is any action that could result in adverse consequences. Fear of adverse consequences is the major deterrent to taking risks. It's a defensive reaction, which does not help people move forward. Obviously, it is in your best interest as a manager to reduce or even eliminate that fear among your employees. How you do that depends on the individual risks with which you're concerned.

Foremost for managers are often the risks of delegating.

Delegating Is Actually a Dual Task

When you delegate an assignment or a project, you incur the risk that your nominee may lack the appropriate skills or knowledge to fulfill your expectations. For you to feel comfortable delegating to this person, you must minimize your risk by being sure the employee has the information, resources, and support necessary to carry out the designated task. That is, you must be convinced that you can trust the person to perform.

The employees you choose to put in charge of projects or assignments are also taking a risk. They're not sure how you'll react if they make mistakes. To reduce their fears, you must make it safe for them to take the risk of accepting your assignment.

Before this can happen, it's important that you convince yourself that effective delegation is good business. In your manager's journal, write down the benefits, both to you and to your employees, of delegating responsibilities to them. Be precise about what's in it for you and what's in it for your employees.

How to Minimize the Risks of Delegating

Making those lists in your manager's journal is excellent preparation, but you may still be hesitant about putting someone else in charge of a project. You may well feel that you can do it faster yourself, but that's not what managers do. Managers motivate other people to carry out the tasks while they supervise.

You can reduce your anxiety by satisfactorily answering three pairs of questions about the person you're considering: (1) Does this person have the abilities to handle this project? How do I know? (2) Does this person have the judgment to make the right decisions? How do I know? (3) Does this person have the emotional maturity to overcome barriers that may be encountered along the way? How do I know?

If you have been observing your employees regularly, you'll know when they are ready to step up to additional responsibilities.

If you don't know, perhaps you should observe them a little more closely before you set up any new opportunity. It is always preferable to delay delegating and thereby increase the probability of success than to guess and be wrong. An error here could hurt both you and your employee, so don't act in haste.

If your answers to the three sets of questions are positive, you can be reasonably sure you will be delegating to the right person. Your next step is to minimize your employees' risk of assuming the responsibility you are about to delegate.

Minimizing Your Employees' Risks

Once again, try to visit the situation from your employees' perspective by answering this question: Under what conditions would I be reluctant to accept a responsibility given to me by my manager? Write your responses in your manager's journal.

For most people, the reluctance ultimately stems from fear, and fear can paralyze. Thus, you need to minimize fearful reactions in your employees in order to enable them to take risks.

Give employees permission to make mistakes by telling them to let you know if they need help, and don't reprimand them if they do. None of us performs perfectly or in the most efficient manner the first time we attempt anything new. Your employees are adults and deserve to be treated as such. Abusive language will provoke ill feelings, which will then restrict their willingness to risk anything.

Encourage them to take chances and to try bigger ones, and don't make them feel guilty if a chance they took didn't pay off. Start with smaller, more familiar tasks in order to ensure success. Being successful from the onset will give them more confidence to continue to try new, unfamiliar activities. If employees err in the assignment, help them understand what went wrong, and then give them another task or project. Even a failure is a valuable experience, since it shows the employee what not to do the next time. In short, don't penalize employees for taking risks.

Recall how you responded when you were a child and one of your parents asked you if you did something that you knew was a no-no, and you were guilty. Whether or not you told the truth probably depended on how your parent had reacted to you previously under similar circumstances. If you had previously told the truth and were severely chastised for your actions, you learned that the truth can hurt. On the other hand, if they appreciated the truth even though they disapproved of the action, and they told you so, you learned that telling the truth is the right thing to do. Be a good authority figure to your employees by extending both guidance and support while you give them direction and latitude.

Delegating Effectively

To delegate effectively, you must first realize that you're not just doling out work to employees and telling them to complete it. You're placing employees in charge of a project and giving them the responsibility for achieving an objective that you consider important. They need to understand and accept this premise before they can take on added responsibility. When you delegate, you share responsibility for outcomes. Help your employees understand the significance of their central roles and of your supporting role. You will help, and they will perform; you will coach, and they will complete.

Second, tell employees to whom you delegate what you want accomplished, and then invite them to decide how to do it. Although their way of proceeding may differ from your approach, the difference is irrelevant as long as they accomplish what you want in a timely manner. By allowing employees to come up with their own solutions or approaches, you're in effect saying, "It's your responsibility; you own it, and I trust you to do the quality job I know you are capable of performing."

If it's appropriate, ask the employee to come up with a written plan for doing the project. Writing out a plan often helps people clarify their purpose and even identify potential trouble spots before they start out. That will further tip the balance toward success. The more the employee knows in advance, the better the performance will be.

Finally, establish follow-up checkpoints. In these meetings, you ascertain how the project is progressing, discuss any aspects of the assignment that may be confusing or need adjustment, and provide whatever other aid the employee may need from you. Your attitude when setting up these checkpoints should be that, as a manager, you have a vested interest in the success of the project, and the employee should view you as a consultant who is there to help him or her succeed.

One word of caution: Do not fall into the trap of micromanaging projects. Don't be like the parent who says to a child, "I trust you to cross the street by yourself, but just to be sure you're doing it right, let me hold your hand." Your employees do not need hand-holding once you've put them in charge of a project. What they need is your trust and the knowledge that you are available to assist when necessary. They don't need or want you to hover over them. Help them think through options, and encourage them to trust themselves.

Coach Employees to Excel

A student we know who was a top player on his school's basketball team suddenly stopped taking long shots or even short jump shots. He began limiting himself to the low-risk layup shots. After several such games, a confused observer asked him why he was taking only sure shots. He said, "Wouldn't you do the same if every time you missed a shot, the coach yelled at you? I just became afraid of taking chances. The price of taking a shot and risking missing it was just too great."

By not making it safe for this excellent athlete to take risks, the coach inadvertently discouraged him from playing his best game. You can avoid making the mistake this coach did by adopting these guidelines:

- Don't cause your employees to avoid taking reasonable risks. Encourage them to take chances, but be sure they are protected. They should be able to see the safety net.

- Invite your employees to state opinions, to give gifts of criticism to you and fellow employees, to ask questions, and to offer recommendations. Thank them for their contributions. Use the listening and questioning techniques from previous chapters in order to make this a true dialogue between you and your employees.

- Make sure your invitations for comment are sincere. Don't tarnish them by making employees feel sorry they opened their mouths. Don't reject any criticism without first giving it ample thought.

- Allow your employees to stick their necks out without fear of having their heads chopped off. This feeling of security will come if there is continuing dialogue. Employees need time to develop trust in you.

- Respond to requests and reasonable favors in a way that doesn't make employees regret having asked you.
- Do whatever you can to gain your employees' trust.

Please note that this chapter advocates taking *reasonable* risks. Remember Larry and his daughter? If the car had been heading for a cliff, he would have inserted himself into the situation immediately, because that would have been a risk with dire consequences. Intervention would have been necessary in that case, but it certainly wasn't necessary just because she was going to miss an exit.

Allow your employees to try new things, while being watchful for inappropriate risks. Encourage employees to work with you, not just for you, by sharing your perceptions of what has to be done and then letting them select a plan of action. Although you may know one way to accomplish the task, it may not be the only or best way.

Delegation itself is a simple process. Everyone involved must have the same goal, and it's up to you as the manager to articulate the goal so that everyone has it straight, set up checkpoints, and give employees the green light to pursue the assigned project. All of this requires open and positive dialogue, and that means talking, listening, and responding appropriately to others.

The Role of Exemplars

If employees feel as strongly about the department and the goal as you do, they will feel comfortable and will rise to the challenge you set. You cultivate that feeling through your own performance. You must delegate because you can't do it all. Let others assume responsibilities they can handle, and give them the space to figure out how to fulfill them. Of course, they won't do everything right all of the time, but neither would you. When you and they join forces, you'll build a bond of trust and respect within the department. When someone makes a mistake, you should acknowledge it, but you don't have to support it. Your employees can learn to live with a flub, but they need the encouragement and freedom to seek better solutions, and they will if you model that behavior for them.

Discovery Lesson

1. Complete the following sentence: "I would be more willing to take reasonable risks if my boss _____."

    Now answer this question: What do I have to do to make it safe for my employees to take reasonable risks?

2. The next time a departmental decision has to be made regarding an isolated task, ask for suggestions from your staff rather than dictating the solution. Choose a relatively safe subject, such as making a schedule, rotating department assignments, or setting up a display. Set the goals for the assignment, and then stand back to give employees room to respond. It may take a little time for them to assume that first risk, but once they start, they will continue.

    Provide guidance on how to implement the called-for action or resolve the conflict, and then support and enable the employees' decision as long as it addresses the goals you had in mind. Even if they decide on something different from your preference, endorse it if it accomplishes the objective. Problems typically allow for many different answers, and your staff just might sprout a great idea that wouldn't have occurred to you. When this happens, it reflects well on your employees and on you.

Use the example of your own best manager as your model of how to delegate and engender risk taking. Think about what impressed you the most in working for this person, and record your conclusions in your journal to remind you as time goes by. It's most likely your best manager practiced the principles advocated in this chapter. Learn from the people you rate as the best, and you just might avoid some of the trial and error that led them to their designation as successful managers.

This new behavior on your part is going to require practice. The accompanying two-part Discovery Lesson will help you understand the behavior changes needed for you to become comfortable with the approach and then put it to the test.

Managing is all about getting others to carry out responsibilities. Your application of the formulas and experiences covered in this chapter will aid you in accomplishing the dual obligation of effectively delegating work to others and providing your employees with an environment that allows them to realize their fullest potential. In this way, the working relationship between manager and employee is structured for the benefit of all parties.

Questions to Consider

- *What are the benefits, both to me and to my employees, of delegating responsibilities?*

- *What can I do to show my employees that I want to protect them from hurting themselves? What kind of safety net can I spread?*

- *Why would my employees be reluctant to accept the responsibilities that I give them?*

- *Why would I be reluctant to accept responsibilities that my manager gives me?*

As a manager, you are only as good as the people under your influence. Hire the best and treat them well to reap the most benefits from your employees.

15

Hire the Right People

WITHOUT A GOOD TEAM OF EMPLOYEES to help you carry out your responsibilities, you're at risk of not fulfilling your ambition to be a successful, professional manager. Just as a good gardener must pick the right seeds and soil and create the right conditions, you must pick the right people and create the conditions for them to grow.

Identifying the right people for your department depends on what you want to accomplish and what kind of work you are doing. For any position you want to fill, you must first clearly define the job requirements for yourself. Only after you have a firm concept of what a particular job is about can you select the best person for it. This is an expertise that you must develop.

Hone Your Skills Before You Need Them

Hiring the best person for a job starts by delineating exactly what the person must be able to do to perform the job most efficiently and effectively. The best way to know what you are looking for is to write down exactly what you expect of the person who will fill the position, because you can't fool the discipline of "talking to" the blank piece of paper. To see for yourself the value of writing down your expectations, complete the following exercise in your manager's journal.

Pick a position within your department and write down the job skills and knowledge that you think are required to do this job well. Then, ask people in the department who occupy a similar position what skills and knowledge they need to do their jobs well. Since they are so close to the real task, they can tell you exactly what it requires. Check your list of what you thought against the list of requirements identified by the workers, and modify your list if necessary. Working from this detailed description of the job requirements, compose several questions that would be appropriate to ask applicants to determine if they possess the identified skills and qualities needed to succeed in this job.

This might seem like a lot of busywork, but this discipline could save you considerable difficulty, and money, in the long run. We've all heard that time is money, but many managers don't heed the implications of that expression. It sounds good, but often it doesn't change any behavior. As a new manager, you should pay especially close attention to how you use your time and the time of your employees.

Hiring staff is typically a significant part of a manager's responsibility, and with every hire, you must do it right the first time in order to gain optimum productivity. If you make a bad hire, the person probably won't last very long on the job, and you'll have to go through the process all over again. This is a poor use of time and is expensive to boot.

According to the U.S. Department of Labor, "A bad hire will cost a company the equivalent of that employee's salary for a six-month period." It certainly won't take very many of these to have a serious impact on your bottom line. A bad hire can be a substantial mistake, but it's one you can avoid by using your professional skills. Try the suggested exercise with a few people in your department now. Don't wait until there is an actual position to be filled. This allows you to practice first and perform later. Your strategy is to hone your skills before you need them in an actual situation.

Again, be specific about what you want to accomplish, and then practice, practice, practice. Too many managers shoot from the hip or act on instinct. If you do either of these, you might be lucky and make a good hiring decision, but it's more likely you'll make an expensive error.

Basic Steps to Good Hiring

Armed with a detailed, clear synopsis of what is required of a candidate to fill a specified position, you're ready to proceed, with care, to the next step.

Announcing the Job

Companies must comply with a host of laws, rules, and regulations regarding the posting of job vacancies in order to provide equal employment opportunities. Talk with your human resources staff to get their input on the appropriate procedures for your company and department. The best advice is know the law and, if you don't know, ask.

Several avenues are open to you for identifying and selecting the best candidate for a position. You may announce the position through whatever forms are appropriate for your company, association, or profession.

Perhaps someone in your department or elsewhere in your organization is interested in the job. Because managers work closely with their employees, they often see those employees in a specific role and assume they wouldn't be interested in a different position. This can be a costly oversight. Managers sometimes just don't think about their staffs' career paths or encourage employees to move up or on to another position. This is how good talent gets lost, so be sure to inform employees of upcoming opportunities, and be supportive of their efforts to grow. That will be good for them, for you, and for the organization.

Screening Applicants

When the job posting is distributed, you'll probably get plenty of applications and résumés. They are your primary sources of information about the candidates' work experience, abilities, and skills. When you review the submissions, write down what you have learned about the candidates and what specific actions they have accomplished. Many résumés contain an extraordinary amount of information, some of which you don't need or want, so list only the facts that relate to the abilities you're looking for in the ideal candidate.

Think: Ready–Willing–Able

Ready, willing, and able are the guiding qualities of the candidate selection process. Looking first at the *able* category, your careful review of the résumés and applications will indicate if the required abilities are present. This is the easiest part of the process, since a candidate either has them or doesn't.

Next comes verification, which is a bit more complicated because applicants sometimes exaggerate their skills and duties on résumés, and you have to check that the facts are as stated. You know what applicants say they are able to do, but you have to be sure the words are truly matched by the deeds. You must verify what you think you learned about a candidate from the written document, and that comes during the interview.

Conducting the Interview

As with formulating the position description, conducting a successful interview involves planning and practice. You will probably spend twenty to fifty minutes with an applicant, and you must know how to gain the insight you need. To prepare, review Chapter 11 on the art of asking questions, and then write down the key questions you will ask at the interviews you conduct.

Verifying Abilities

The right questions will flesh out the applicant's abilities and produce examples that demonstrate those abilities. Matching your questions to the precise set of skills that the position requires will keep the interview from straying off target.

Keep questions geared to the requirements you articulated, and don't be satisfied with superficial comments. To get at the information you need, you have to probe deeply without coming across as an interrogator. Incorporate the questioning skills you've learned, and remember to take advantage of all of the appropriate techniques, including open questions, closed questions, probes, echoes, and follow-up questions. When you ask for and receive detailed examples of stated accomplishments, you will be more comfortable with your final hiring decision.

From Able to Willing

The interview will also help you determine if the applicant is *willing* to fulfill the responsibilities of the job. Unlike the tangible abilities, these are intangible personal qualities and are a little more difficult to pin down. How willing is the applicant to take charge, study, and learn new skills? Is the person flexible? Is the person a self-starter? Will he or she share information? Can he or she accept correction and direction? Will the applicant go the extra mile, help coworkers, take responsibility, and show initiative?

The answers are often gleaned from more pointed questions about the applicant's job experience. This is a time in which the active listening skills you developed in Chapter 5 will come in handy. You will be able to read and interpret clues that indicate if the candidate possesses the intangible willing skills that make for a good hire. For example, the candidate's description of skills learned in a previous job can disclose how little or how much the person grew in his or her previous position. If the candidate asks about training programs and schedules for training, this suggests a desire to continue to learn and lack of contentment with a rote job. From an applicant's description of committee work, you can deduce that the person is a team player and cooperates with fellow employees.

Always seek out evidence and documentation of these intangibles in action. Don't simply accept a generality such as "I welcome challenges." Uncover incidences that support the statement. One way of doing this is to ask candidates to tell you about a challenge they undertook and describe how they handled it. Apply the appropriate questioning techniques, and anytime you hear a generalization or an abstraction, probe for concrete examples. This way, you keep achievements at the forefront and won't get caught up in vagaries. You are going to hire the best candidate to perform a certain function, not just the best talker.

With this dynamic, in addition to answering your questions, prospective employees have a chance to stand out and to tell their complete stories when they might otherwise have been too nervous to summon up details. They will see that your interest is in their performance and that you want to know about them. This demonstrates to interviewees that you value them as people and as prospective employees.

From Willing to Ready

You can determine if an applicant is *ready* for the position at hand by identifying past patterns and using them to deduce the next stage in the person's professional development. By using the suggested questioning and listening techniques, you can learn much about the whole person, including personality and personal qualifications. You will want to take into consideration whether or not a candidate seems to have grown in past jobs. Has the person taken on ever-increasing responsibilities? Does the person display sufficient maturity to relate to a diverse group of coworkers?

Ultimately, you have to determine if the applicant will fit well with the departmental culture you've worked so hard to create. That doesn't mean that the individual has to be exactly like everyone else on your team, but all new hires should be compatible with those already in place. Benchmark candidates against the qualities you consider valuable to your department.

Targeting Scenarios to Generate Dialogue

Here are sample questions you might pose that will help to divulge how ready, willing, and able an applicant is:

- If you could have the most ideal job at this time in your life, what would that job be, and what are the qualities that make that job ideal? Why do you feel you are qualified for it? In what ways have you exhibited the skills and traits that make you qualified for this job?

- Think of the best manager you ever had. What qualities made this person the best manager in your eyes? Do you possess any of these qualities? If so, when and how did you use those qualities? What are some of the qualities that the manager possessed that you wish you had or would like to improve upon?

- Think of the worst manager you ever had. What qualities made this person the worst manager in your eyes? Which of those qualities do you possess? Have you ever demonstrated those qualities? If so, what was the circumstance?

These questions are designed to instigate conversation and reveal elements of the candidate's personality. You could also describe a problem that you encountered in your department and ask applicants how they would handle it. Be sure to develop a dialogue; don't simply invite applicants to deliver a long speech, since they might be unsure of what kind of information you want. Don't ask applicants to envision a scenario that is so general and open-ended that they don't even know where to begin. Applicants are typically so nervous that this kind of conversational obfuscation could leave them disconcerted and leave you without answers.

In your manager's journal, try to brainstorm other thought-provoking questions or conversations that will help reveal how ready, willing, and able an applicant is.

Every Step Counts

To put you on solid footing before you must set out on an employee search, this final section recaps the important elements of the hiring process. First, be sure you know the exact skills required for the position. If you're thorough in your evaluation of the necessary skills and traits, you will be able to quickly conclude if candidates are likely to possess these skills, both from their résumés and during the interviews. If you don't know exactly what you want, you won't know if the candidate has it. Request the input and perspective of employees who hold or have held a similar position. Various points of view will assist you in developing a targeted job description.

When screening and interviewing prospective employees, concentrate on the ready, willing, and able items. Settling in to an easy and engaging conversation could distract you from your mission, which is to glean information pertinent to the candidate's ability to do the job and to do it well. Review the chapters on listening and asking questions before you hold interviews. By taking time and care to prepare, you avoid the high costs of a bad hire and the revolving door of employees.

Questions to Consider

- *What are the actual skills needed to perform each of the jobs in my department?*

- *Who can help me get a clear understanding of what is really needed by people in my department?*

- *If and when I have to hire someone new for the department, how can I find applicants? Where can I interview them? How can I evaluate and compare candidates?*

You gain confidence by consistently doing the right things in appropriate ways.

Really big people—those whose spirit matches their stature—find time to do things for others, little things that clearly say, "I genuinely care about you."

16

Moving Forward

MANAGERS MUST KNOW AS MUCH as possible about their employees, help them recognize their abilities, and guide them to perform to their maximum potential so that they benefit the organization and themselves. This book sets forth the basic principles, tools, and guidance you need to become a successful, professional manager. The rest is up to you.

You have broad and varied responsibilities within the work environment, but your influence goes far beyond the workplace. Always remember that your behavior affects the lives of other people in a profound way.

In whatever you do—hire, fire, promote, transfer, counsel, correct, support, coach, guide, or discipline—keep in mind what impact you may have on the lives of others. Your employees have bills to pay, plans to complete, trips to take, dreams to ponder. How you treat them at work influences all of these acts. Do your job—that's what you get paid for—but do it with sensitivity and humanity.

Being sensitive doesn't make you a weak manager who is too easily influenced. On the contrary, there will be many days when you must do what is unpopular, when you have to say no, but you can do it in ways that will not be personally hurtful and that even are potentially helpful. Even bad news can be delivered in a manner that is not harsh or vicious. A thorough explanation can often avert future problems.

Some managers enjoy seeing themselves as tough as nails, and in some companies, that behavior might even be rewarded. You can make tough decisions, but your demeanor doesn't have to be tough. When you have to say no, think through your options for delivering the message and the impact it will have. Instead of a simple "No," will your employees hear "Absolutely not!" or a regretful "Unfortunately not"? You have dozens of ways to communicate the same information while sending vastly different messages. Take care to send the exact messages you intend, and anticipate the consequences of your messages. Managing excellence requires open and constant positive communication. Think about not only the substance but also how you package it. Where, when, and how you deliver information can be more significant than the words.

This book has repeatedly highlighted the stature of honor and respect. Everything you do as a manager you do with and through other people. You now are better equipped with skills, techniques, strategies, and plans that will help you effectively interact with a disparate collection of individuals. In addition, your job requires that you eye the hard realities of profits, schedules, regulations, distribution, production, and a host of other demands. All of these elements, from people to profits, have to be balanced. Every facet of work, from the moment you walk in to the moment you leave, has to be managed within the framework of the people involved in making your business or department run smoothly and profitably.

Being promoted to manager is exciting and rewarding, but it also imposes an awesome responsibility because of the influence and impact you have on the lives of many people. If you carry out the job with care, you will do it well.

Once again . . . Congratulations on your promotion to manager, and good luck!

Appendix

We have pulled key points from the text for you to photocopy and frame or distribute to your employees.

What I Get Paid to Do

- I get paid to create a department in which we all feel motivated to be the best we can be.
- I get paid to encourage everyone to cooperate with one another so we can achieve our department's objectives.
- I get paid to ensure that we all abide by the ideals and standards that define our department.

Essentials for Managerial Excellence

- Be sensitive to people's feelings, and be kind to them.
- Take time to make people feel special.
- Listen to people's emotions as well as words.
- View people's needs and wants as valid.
- Choose your battles wisely.
- Respect people's differences.
- Avoid being defensive and placing people on the defensive.
- Give people the benefit of the doubt.
- Resolve interpersonal problems as quickly as possible, preferably before parting for any significant time.
- In short, treat people the way you would like to be treated: as a valued friend.
- Finally, never take people for granted—never.

An attitude is a state of mind and a predisposition to actions based on what you tell yourself.

The Three Elements of Attitudes

1. What you tell yourself
2. Your state of mind resulting from what you tell yourself
3. Actions that stem from what you tell yourself, combined with your state of mind

To change an attitude, you must alter what you tell yourself.

Encourage Positive Attitudes

Positive attitudes lead to productive actions;
negative attitudes lead to unproductive actions.

Being an Excellent Manager Begins with Being a Good Person—a Mensch

A mensch is a respectful and genuine person who is sensitive and appropriately responsive to others' feelings.

A mensch exhibits, embodies, and consistently adheres to and advocates the following principles, attitudes, and behaviors in dealings with people:

- Be a perpetual student and learn from everyone, regardless of education, age, position, or status.
- In your desire to understand people, ask appropriate questions, in an appropriate way, at an appropriate time, and in an appropriate place.
- Act responsibly and kindly toward yourself and others.
- Listen attentively to what people say, both verbally and nonverbally, and respond appropriately to their messages.
- Demonstrate a genuine regard for all people's feelings, and accept those feelings as being valid.
- Be sensitively forthright and honest with people, leaving little to the fate of imagination and confusion.
- Don't allow defensiveness to dictate actions; all actions should be guided by a desire to be helpful and cooperative.
- Make people feel valued by asking for their opinions, requesting their help, praising commendable performance, and being polite and courteous at all times.

In short, by being considerate, righteous, and positive in your dealings with people, a mensch builds healthy communication bridges.

How Do You Make Your Employees Feel?

People may forget what you said;
they may even forget what you did;
but rarely, if ever, will they forget
how you made them feel.

The Problem-Solving Process

When faced with a problem, ask:

- What specifically do I want? Is it reasonable (i.e., attainable)?
- Do I have a detailed plan for achieving my reasonable wants? If I anticipate barriers that could interfere with reaching my objectives, does my plan describe how I could overcome those barriers?
- Am I committed to working through my plan methodically and conscientiously?
- How will I determine whether or not I'm on track? How frequently should I follow up?
- If negative thoughts or outside influences are sidetracking me, what specifically can I do to rid myself of those thoughts and influences?

Characteristics of a Departmental Weed

A weed is any action or reaction that

- does not contribute to the betterment of our department
- does not reflect our mission statement
- undermines problem solving
- hurts the department as a whole or any individual

About the Authors

Jack H. Grossman, Ph.D., is the author of six books and Executive Mentor and Professor Emeritus at DePaul University's Kellstadt Graduate School of Business in Chicago. Throughout his career, he has helped CEOs and line-level managers develop the art of creating and maintaining cooperative relationships in both their personal and professional lives. Dr. Grossman and his associates have decades of experience providing interpersonal mentoring and business analysis services across the country. He resides with his wife of forty-five years in Deerfield, Illinois.

J. Robert Parkinson, Ph.D., is a member of the faculty of Northwestern University in Evanston, Illinois, and a consultant and trainer specializing in effective communication for major corporations, professional associations, and government agencies. The author of five books, he has served as the on-air host of numerous radio and television programs.

Dr. Parkinson provides a wide variety of professional services to organizations and individuals across the United States. He conducts seminars and personal coaching and counseling sessions in relationship building, management practices, and communication techniques. His professional activities have included extensive travel throughout the country as well as Europe, South America, Africa, and Australia. With his wife, Eileen, he divides his time between homes in Glenview, Illinois, and Sarasota, Florida.

For further information about the authors' backgrounds and their respective services, please contact them at:

www.Managingothers.com